Everyday Spelling

Practice Masters

6

Scott Foresman
Addison Wesley

Editorial Offices: Glenview, Illinois • Menlo Park, California
Sales Offices: Reading, Massachusetts • Atlanta, Georgia • Glenview, Illinois
Carrollton, Texas • Menlo Park, California

1-800-552-2259
http://www.sf.aw.com

D0874922

ISBN: 0-673-28993-1

Copyright © 1998
Addison-Wesley Educational Publishers Inc.
All rights reserved.
Printed in the United States of America.

45678910-PT-05040302010099

CONTENTS

Everyday Spelling © Scott Foresman • Addison Wesley

CONTENTS

CONTENTS

CONTENTS

Everyday Spelling © Scott Foresman • Addison Wesley

Name _____

Challenge Words

preliminary   tremendous   mediocre   perception   neutrality

■ Use Challenge Words to complete the puzzle. Fill in the letters going down to spell the word meaning "average."

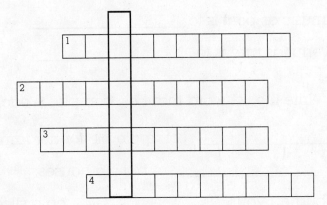

Across
1. huge
2. before starting
3. understanding
4. policy of not being on anyone's side

■ Have you ever seen something that turned out to be different from what you expected? Think about an experience that surprised you in that way. Write a paragraph about it, using one or more Challenge Words.

_____

_____

_____

_____

_____

_____

_____

_____

1 ■ THINK AND PRACTICE

| poetry | beautiful | thirteen | tongue | pieces |
| neighborhood | thousand | through | unusual | building |

■ **Analogies** Write the list word that completes each analogy.

1. Bad is to good as ugly is to _____.

2. Twig is to nest as brick is to _____.

3. Composer is to music as poet is to _____.

4. Strong is to powerful as rare is to _____.

■ **Context Clues** Write the list word that best completes each sentence.

5. Marla cut six _____ of apple pie for her family.

6. Jesse lives in a _____ of big old houses.

7. Have you ever burned your _____ on a slice of pizza?

8. Viking explorers came to America a _____ years ago.

9. In English we read the _____ of Robert Frost.

10. The American flag once had _____ stars.

11. Snow in September is an _____ sight.

STRATEGIC SPELLING: Developing Spelling Consciousness

We sometimes misspell familiar words that we shouldn't miss. Proofread the passage. Find the four misspelled words and write them correctly.

It's been six weeks since we moved here, and I guess it's not so bad. We ride our bikes throw the park every day. The flowers in the park are beutiful! I like our apartment biulding. I miss my friend Shannon, but she said she would come visit when I turn thriteen.

12. _____   14. _____

13. _____   15. _____

Everyday Spelling © Scott Foresman • Addison Wesley

Word List

poetry	beautiful	thirteen	tongue	pieces
neighborhood	thousand	through	unusual	building
license	remodel	grateful	enemy	instrument
perform	prefer	judged	adjusted	soldier

■ **Word Math** Answer each problem with a list word.

1. streets + house + people = ___
2. driver + legal + document = ___
3. rhyme + verse + similes = ___
4. vase + drop + shatter = ___
5. mouth + talk + taste = ___
6. tune + practice + music = ___
7. ten + two + one = ___
8. act + dance + sing = ___
9. weird + strange + uncommon = ___
10. contest + entrants + selected = ___
11. war + uniform + army = ___
12. finished + done + completed = ___

■ **Riddles** Write a list word to match each clue. HINT: Use the sentence meaning and the underlined words as clues.

13. There are many, many grains of <u>sand</u>.
14. I'm so glad I <u>ate</u> before the game.
15. We <u>just</u> fixed the picture on the TV set.
16. Today we will <u>be</u> at the spectacular art show.
17. <u>My</u> former friend is not welcome here.
18. I will <u>refer</u> you to another doctor if you wish.
19. We will use this <u>model</u> when we restore the house.
20. The <u>din</u> from the construction site was deafening.

1. _____
2. _____
3. _____
4. _____
5. _____
6. _____
7. _____
8. _____
9. _____
10. _____
11. _____
12. _____
13. _____
14. _____
15. _____
16. _____
17. _____
18. _____
19. _____
20. _____

1 ■ REVIEW

Word List

poetry	beautiful	thirteen	tongue	pieces
neighborhood	thousand	through	unusual	building
license	remodel	grateful	enemy	instrument
perform	prefer	judged	adjusted	soldier

■ **Antonyms** Write the list word that completes each phrase.

1. not *around*, but ___
2. not *friend*, but ___
3. not *dislike*, but ___
4. not *ugly*, but ___

■ **Associations** Write the list word that is associated with each word below.

5. act   9. war
6. teenager   10. orchestra
7. roof   11. puzzle
8. driving   12. taste

■ **Classifying** Write the list word that belongs in each group.

13. redo, rebuild, ___
14. aligned, reset, ___
15. rhyme, verse, ___
16. ten, hundred, ___

■ **Words in Context** Complete the sentence with words from the box.

judged	grateful
neighborhood	unusual

The (17) defendant was relieved when the jury (18) that she was innocent of any wrongdoing in the (19) traffic accident that happened in the (20) of the school.

1. _____
2. _____
3. _____
4. _____
5. _____
6. _____
7. _____
8. _____
9. _____
10. _____
11. _____
12. _____
13. _____
14. _____
15. _____
16. _____
17. _____
18. _____
19. _____
20. _____

Everyday Spelling © Scott Foresman • Addison Wesley

Challenge Words

adequate   reconcile   insulation   thunderstorm   reluctant

■ Use Challenge Words to complete the relationships described below.

1. Lining is to coat as _____ is to house.

2. Blizzard is to snowfall as _____ is to rain shower.

3. Delicious is to good-tasting as _____ is to good enough.

4. Estrange is to _____ as fight is to make up.

5. Unwilling is to _____ as eager is to expectant.

■ Did you ever try fixing something? Sometimes it's easy; sometimes it's impossible. Use Challenge Words to write a paragraph about the frustration or satisfaction of doing repairs on your own.

_____

_____

_____

_____

_____

_____

_____

Everyday Spelling © Scott Foresman • Addison Wesley

2 ■ THINK AND PRACTICE

admire	canyon	lemonade	method	distance
swimming	modern	comedy	husband	clumsy

■ Antonyms Write the list word that means the opposite
of each word.

1. old-fashioned   _____

2. tragedy   _____

3. dislike   _____

4. graceful   _____

■ Analogies Write the list word that completes each analogy.

5. *Woman* is to *wife* as *man* is to _____.

6. *Track* is to *running* as *pool* is to _____.

7. *Oranges* are to *orange juice* as *lemons* are to _____.

8. *High* is to *mountain* as *deep* is to _____.

9. *Quart* is to *volume* as *mile* is to _____.

10. *Cry* is to *tragedy* as *laugh* is to _____.

11. *Magical* is to *magic* as *methodical* is to _____.

12. *Deer* is to *graceful* as *bull* is to _____.

STRATEGIC SPELLING: Seeing Meaning Connections
Complete each sentence with a word from the box.

Words related to *admire*		
admirable	admiration	admirer

13. William is a great _____ of Jackie Joyner-Kersee.

14. He thinks her athletic skills are _____.

15. William expressed his _____ in a letter.

Everyday Spelling © Scott Foresman • Addison Wesley

Name _____

Word List

admire	canyon	lemonade	method	distance
swimming	modern	comedy	husband	clumsy
magnify	cannon	decorate	strict	injury
tissue	honesty	property	hundredth	dungeon

■ **Classifying** Write the list word that belongs in each group below.

1. land, estate, ___
2. fracture, wound, ___
3. soda, milkshake, ___
4. tragedy, melodrama, ___
5. floating, diving, ___
6. respect, approve, ___
7. cellar, cavern, ___
8. musket, artillery, ___
9. wife, daughter, ___
10. tenth, fiftieth, ___

1. _____
2. _____
3. _____
4. _____
5. _____
6. _____
7. _____
8. _____
9. _____
10. _____

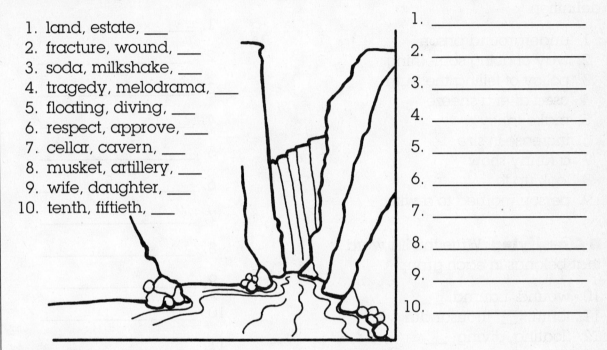

■ **Words in Context** Write a list word to complete each sentence.

11. Which _____ do you use to study for tests?

12. The runner ran the entire _____ in one hour.

13. Sal felt _____ when he kept tripping on his laces.

14. Can you help me _____ the gym for the dance?

15. Maya's mother is very _____ about Maya's homework.

16. Dinosaurs are extinct in the _____ world.

17. Rescuers brought the injured hiker up out of the _____.

18. Carlos took off his stage makeup with a _____.

19. Use the lens to _____ this small writing.

20. Jake's principles include _____ and loyalty.

2 ■ REVIEW

Word List

admire	canyon	lemonade	method	distance
swimming	modern	comedy	husband	clumsy
magnify	cannon	decorate	strict	injury
tissue	honesty	property	hundredth	dungeon

■ **Definitions** Write the list word that fits each definition.

1. underground prison
2. way of doing something
3. policy of telling the truth
4. used after a sneeze
5. make fancy
6. increase in size
7. a funny show
8. look up to
9. person married to a wife

■ **Classifying** Write the list word that belongs in each group.

10. wound, trauma, ___
11. tenth, ___, thousandth
12. floating, diving, ___
13. new, innovative, ___
14. limeade, orangeade, ___
15. awkward, gawky, ___
16. harsh, severe, ___
17. valley, gorge, ___
18. far, away, ___
19. gun, artillery, ___
20. possession, ownership, ___

1. _____
2. _____
3. _____
4. _____
5. _____
6. _____
7. _____
8. _____
9. _____
10. _____
11. _____
12. _____
13. _____
14. _____
15. _____
16. _____
17. _____
18. _____
19. _____
20. _____

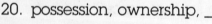

Everyday Spelling © Scott Foresman • Addison Wesley

Challenge Words
deceitful   retrieval   conceivable   unwieldy   grievance

■ Write a Challenge Word to complete each equation.

1. take back + act of doing something = _____

2. not + easily managed = _____

3. lies + filled with = _____

4. understand + able to = _____

5. mourn + action or quality of = _____

■ Friends and neighbors can get into some ridiculous disagreements. Use one or more Challenge Words to write a newspaper article about a real or imagined disagreement.

_____

_____

_____

_____

_____

_____

_____

_____

Everyday Spelling © Scott Foresman • Addison Wesley

3 ■ THINK AND PRACTICE

ceiling	receipt	deceive	neither	field
achieve	belief	brief	relief	apiece

■ **Synonyms** Write a list word that means the same as the underlined word.

1. The children flew their kites in a big <u>meadow</u>. _____

2. The roses cost one dollar <u>each</u>. _____

3. Paula's campaign speech was very <u>short</u>. _____

4. Juan is very nice. Don't let his harsh manner <u>fool</u> you.

   _____

5. Mr. Wood has a strong <u>idea</u> that there is life on Mars.

   _____

■ **Context Clues** Write the list word that completes each sentence.

6. Noriko gave the man a _____ for the doll he bought.

7. _____ Tim nor Rob tried out for the basketball team.

8. A rain shower brought _____ from the summer heat.

9. A college education will help you _____ your goals.

10. Cara hung a piñata from the _____ of her room.

11. The farmer planted corn in his _____.

STRATEGIC SPELLING: Using the Problem Parts Strategy
Write four list words that are hard for you. Underline the part
of each word that gives you problems. Picture the words.
Focus on the problem parts.

12. _____   14. _____

13. _____   15. _____

Everyday Spelling © Scott Foresman • Addison Wesley

Name _____

Word List

ceiling	receipt	deceive	neither	field
achieve	belief	brief	relief	apiece
leisure	protein	receiver	seize	conceited
shield	niece	diesel	grief	yield

■ **Long e** Write the list word that fits each clue below. HINT: All the list words in each group should rhyme with one another.

1. a strong conviction about something
2. extreme sadness
3. not lasting very long
4. something that removes pain
_____
5. a plot of open land
6. to protect someone from something
7. to give way
_____
8. each; for each one
9. the daughter of one's brother or sister
_____
10. to fool or mislead
11. to reach one's goal

1. _____

2. _____

3. _____

4. _____

5. _____

6. _____

7. _____

8. _____

9. _____

10. _____

11. _____

■ **Puzzle** Use the printed letters as clues and write a list word in each set of blanks.

12. __ __ __ __ __ **v** __ __

13. __ __ **n** __ __ __

14. __ __ __ **z** __

15. **d** __ __ __ __ __

16. **p** __ __ **t** __ __ __

17. __ __ __ __ __ __ __ **r**

18. __ __ __ __ __ **p** __

19. __ __ __ __ **s** __ __

20. **c** __ __ __ __ __ __ __

3 ■ REVIEW

Word List

ceiling	receipt	deceive	neither	field
achieve	belief	brief	relief	apiece
leisure	protein	receiver	seize	conceited
shield	niece	diesel	grief	yield

■ **Pronunciations** Write a list word for each pronunciation.

1. (ə chēv′) ___
2. (kən sē′tid) ___
3. (ri sē′vər) ___

■ **Making Associations** Write the list word that is associated with each item below.

4. nephew
5. nor
6. engine
7. help
8. vacation
9. armor
10. payment
11. stop
12. wheat

■ **Antonyms** Write the list words that mean the opposite of the underlined words.

13. The floor needed repair.
14. The Smiths are enjoying a long stay at the beach.
15. Happiness overcame Joyce when she heard the unexpected news.
16. His partners tried to tell him honestly about his rights.
17. Dad decided to let go of the ball.

■ **Seeing Meaning Connections** Write the unused list words that fit the definitions.

18. for every one
19. something people accept and trust in
20. a nutritious substance found in foods

1. _____
2. _____
3. _____
4. _____
5. _____
6. _____
7. _____
8. _____
9. _____
10. _____
11. _____
12. _____
13. _____
14. _____
15. _____
16. _____
17. _____
18. _____
19. _____
20. _____

Everyday Spelling © Scott Foresman • Addison Wesley

Challenge Words

curlicue   newcomer   aptitude   ukulele   fugitive

■ Write the Challenge Word that fits each clue listed below.

1. You might find this on someone's writing. _____

2. You might find this at a folk music concert. _____

3. You might find one on the first day of school. _____

4. You might find this in yourself when you try something new.

   _____

5. You might find one hiding aboard a ship. _____

■ Do you dream about solving an international mystery? Use one or more Challenge Words to write a paragraph about a very important detective assignment.

_____

_____

_____

_____

_____

_____

_____

_____

_____

_____

_____

_____

4 ■ THINK AND PRACTICE

| reduce | attitude | sewer | New York | review |
| value | continue | humid | United States | universe |

■ **Context Quotes** Write the list word that is missing from each person's statement.

1. Teacher: "The best students have a positive _____."

2. Weather forecaster: "The first day of summer will be hot and _____."

3. Art dealer: "This painting will increase in _____."

4. Astronomer: "There are many galaxies in the _____."

5. Movie critic: "I often _____ children's movies."

■ **Classifying** Write the word that belongs in each group.

6. drainage, gutter, _____

7. advance, move ahead, _____

8. France, China, _____

9. lessen, decrease, _____

10. Texas, California, _____

11. sticky, muggy, _____

STRATEGIC SPELLING: Seeing Meaning Connections
Write words from the box that fit the definitions.

| Words with *view* | | | |
| review | viewpoint | preview | interview |

12. A meeting at which a reporter gets information is an

    _____.

13. An advance showing of a movie is a _____.

14. A standpoint on a subject is a _____.

15. An evaluation of a book or a play is a _____.

Word List

reduce	attitude	sewer	New York	review
value	continue	humid	United States	universe
costume	absolutely	assume	renew	viewpoint
interview	preview	rescue	uniform	reunion

■ **Words in Context** Write the list word that is missing from each person's statement.

1. Diet Expert: "If you ___ you will be healthier."
2. Magazine Seller: "Would you like to ___ your subscription?"
3. News Reporter: "My ___ with the president went well."
4. Politician: "I will ___ not raise your taxes!"
5. Nurse: "My new ___ has a button missing."
6. Moviegoer: "I hope they show a ___ of the new science fiction show."
7. Writer: "My character lives beneath ___ City."
8. Debate Coach: "Be sure to state your ___ clearly."
9. Newspaper Reader: "I disagree with this movie ___!"
10. Principal: "The class of '47 will hold their ___ next weekend."
11. Tour Director: "We'll fly across the ___ to California."
12. Astronomer: "The ___ is larger than we can imagine!"

■ **Base Words** Write the list word that is the base word for each word below.

13. attitudes
14. continued
15. rescuer
16. costuming
17. assuming
18. valuable
19. sewers
20. humidity

1. _____
2. _____
3. _____
4. _____
5. _____
6. _____
7. _____
8. _____
9. _____
10. _____
11. _____
12. _____
13. _____
14. _____
15. _____
16. _____
17. _____
18. _____
19. _____
20. _____

Everyday Spelling © Scott Foresman • Addison Wesley

Name _____

4 ■ REVIEW

Word List

reduce	attitude	sewer	New York	review
value	continue	humid	United States	universe
costume	absolutely	assume	renew	viewpoint
interview	preview	rescue	uniform	reunion

■ Base Words Write the list word that is the base word of each word below.

1. rescued
2. uniformity
3. humidify
4. continuous
5. universal
6. renewal
7. valuable
8. assuming
9. reducible

■ Analogies Write the list word that completes each analogy.

10. Paper is to trash can as water is to ___.
11. Play is to critique as book is to ___.
12. Family is to gathering as student is to ___.
13. Painter is to coveralls as actor is to ___.
14. Windy City is to Chicago as Big Apple is to ___.
15. Sample is to food as ___ is to movie.
16. Europe is to France as America is to ___.
17. Sincerely is to wholeheartedly as completely is to ___.

■ Exact Meanings Write the list word that makes sense in each sentence below.

18. All the reporters were on hand to ___ the mayor.
19. Success has a lot to do with having a positive ___.
20. The book was written from the author's ___.

1. _____
2. _____
3. _____
4. _____
5. _____
6. _____
7. _____
8. _____
9. _____
10. _____
11. _____
12. _____
13. _____
14. _____
15. _____
16. _____
17. _____
18. _____
19. _____
20. _____

Everyday Spelling © Scott Foresman • Addison Wesley

Challenge Words

| patrolled | patrolling | dignified |
| dignifying | staggered | staggering |

■ Complete the following police report using the correct forms of the Challenge Words.

I was _____ a neighborhood I had often

_____ before, when a _____ old woman

_____ out of a doorway and down the street. She was

carrying a heavy object. I called out to ask whether she needed help, but

she was not _____ my silly question with an answer. So I

walked over to help her. I was shocked to see her stop _____

and start to sprint away! She was none other than Galloping Gabby, that

white-haired Robin Hood of the city.

■ Imagine that Galloping Gabby got caught. Write a paragraph about the scene above from her point of view. Use one or more Challenge Words in your description.

_____

_____

_____

_____

_____

_____

_____

_____

_____

_____

5 ■ THINK AND PRACTICE

answered	answering	decided	deciding	included
including	omitted	omitting	satisfied	satisfying

■ **Complete a Paragraph** Write a list word to complete each sentence in the paragraph.

   Rolanda was (1)_____ which sport to play after school. She wrote down her choices, which (2)_____ soccer and basketball. When her teacher asked which sport she had chosen, she (3)_____ that she wasn't sure. Then she realized she had (4)_____ one sport. Rolanda got her racket and ran to the tennis court, feeling (5)_____ with her choice.

■ **Adding Endings** Write the list words formed by adding **-ed** or **-ing**.

   6. decide + ed _____

   7. omit + ing _____

   8. answer + ing _____

   9. satisfy + ing _____

   10. include + ing _____

STRATEGIC SPELLING: Building New Words
Add **-ed** and **-ing** to each of these words: *prefer, license, magnify, continue,* and *shield.* Remember what you learned.

Add -ed   **Add -ing**

11. _____   _____

12. _____   _____

13. _____   _____

14. _____   _____

15. _____   _____

Everyday Spelling © Scott Foresman • Addison Wesley

Name _____

Word List

answered	answering	decided	deciding	included
including	omitted	omitting	satisfied	satisfying
delayed	delaying	remembered	remembering	exercised
exercising	interfered	interfering	occurred	occurring

■ **Word Forms** Write the list word that makes sense in each sentence and has the same ending as the underlined word.

1. <u>Dieting</u> and ___ often go together.
2. The explosions kept ___ and <u>frightening</u> the town.
3. Our flight was ___ and <u>rerouted</u> because of the storm.
4. That store always has <u>pleased</u> and ___ customers.
5. No one ___ the phone when I <u>called</u>.
6. Grandma was ___ old times and <u>laughing</u> about them.
7. We are <u>packing</u> and ___ several days' clothing.
8. We <u>discussed</u> the test and ___ to study together.
9. The pounding <u>annoyed</u> me and ___ with my sleep.
10. When Nan <u>looked</u> at the empty envelope, she saw that she had ___ the card.

■ **What's Missing?** Write the list word to complete each group below.

11. delay, delayed, ___
12. answer, answered, ___
13. remember, remembering, ___
14. interfere, interfered, ___
15. decide, decided, ___
16. include, including, ___
17. exercise, exercising, ___
18. omit, omitted, ___
19. occur, occurring, ___
20. satisfy, satisfied, ___

1. _____
2. _____
3. _____
4. _____
5. _____
6. _____
7. _____
8. _____
9. _____
10. _____
11. _____
12. _____
13. _____
14. _____
15. _____
16. _____
17. _____
18. _____
19. _____
20. _____

Everyday Spelling © Scott Foresman • Addison Wesley

25

5 ■ REVIEW

Word List

answered	answering	decided	deciding	included
including	omitted	omitting	satisfied	satisfying
delayed	delaying	remembered	remembering	exercised
exercising	interfered	interfering	occurred	occurring

■ **Double Duty** Add two suffixes to each word in parentheses to form list words that complete each sentence.

1–2. (satisfy) To have ___ guests, serve ___ meals.

3–4. (omit) Joe wished he had ___ the salt instead of ___ the cinnamon.

5–6. (exercise) The more they ___, the more they loved ___.

■ **Words That Add Up** Write the list word that has each meaning and ending given below.

7. reply + ed = ___
8. hesitation + ing = ___
9. contain + ed = ___
10. meddle + ing = ___
11. recall + ing = ___
12. happen + ed = ___
13. conclude + ing = ___

■ **Classifying** Write the list word that is most similar in meaning to each word or phrase below.

14. reminisced
15. butted in
16. postponed
17. taking place
18. responding
19. involving
20. determined

1. _____
2. _____
3. _____
4. _____
5. _____
6. _____
7. _____
8. _____
9. _____
10. _____
11. _____
12. _____
13. _____
14. _____
15. _____
16. _____
17. _____
18. _____
19. _____
20. _____

Everyday Spelling © Scott Foresman • Addison Wesley

Name _____

| **Lesson 1** | | | | |
| poetry | thirteen | tongue | neighborhood | building |

■ **Associations** Write the list word that is associated with each item.

1. rhymes _____

2. skyscraper _____

3. taste _____

4. number _____

5. houses _____

| **Lesson 2** | | | | |
| canyon | method | swimming | comedy | husband |

■ **Definitions** Write the list word that is missing from each person's statement.

1. Explorer: "I will hike through this rocky _____."

2. Athlete: "Today I will practice _____ laps."

3. Wife: "I will call my _____."

4. Scientist: "What scientific _____ will I use in this experiment?"

5. Actor: "My next movie is a _____."

| **Lesson 3** | | | | |
| achieve | field | relief | receipt | deceive |

■ **Making Connections** Write the list word that answers each question.

1. What do you get to show you have paid? _____

2. What might a fan give you on a hot day? _____

3. What do people who are not honest do? _____

4. Where does a farmer plant crops? _____

5. What do you do when you accomplish something? _____

6B ■ REVIEW

Lesson 4

reduce	New York	review	continue	United States

■ **Drawing Conclusions** Write the list word that matches each clue.

1. a large city _____

2. a country with fifty states _____

3. to go on _____

4. the opposite of *preview* _____

5. a synonym for *decrease* _____

Lesson 5

answered	deciding	including	satisfied	omitting

■ **Word Forms** For each base word, write the **-ed** or **-ing** form.

Base word	-ed	-ing
1. answer	_____	answering
2. omit	omitted	_____
3. satisfy	_____	satisfying
4. include	included	_____
5. decide	decided	_____

Challenge Words

martial	marshall	bizarre
bazaar	discreet	discrete

■ Answer the clues below to complete each of the puzzles.

Across
1. an official
2. very strange
3. respectful, reserved

Down
1. about war
2. outdoor market
3. separate

■ Travel, whether by plane, car, or imagination, can be exciting. Use one or more Challenge Words to write a paragraph about an exotic place you have visited or read about.

_____

_____

_____

_____

_____

_____

_____

_____

7 ■ THINK AND PRACTICE

their	there	they're	wring	ring
chili	chilly	scent	sent	cent

■ **Definitions** Read each sentence. Write the correct word for each definition.

A chilly fall evening is a good time to eat chili.

    cool   a spicy stew

1. _____   2. _____

Theresa's mom sent her a bouquet with a sweet scent.

    fragrance   had delivered

3. _____   4. _____

They're practicing free throws over there.

    in that place   they are

5. _____   6. _____

■ **Word Choice** Write the correct list word for each sentence.

7. (Ring, Wring) out your swimsuit after you swim.   _____

8. They planted corn in (their, they're) backyard.   _____

9. Kelly (sent, cent) us a postcard from camp.   _____

10. Akiko found a golden (wring, ring) in the park.   _____

11. What can you buy with one (sent, cent)?   _____

12. Nights are (chilly, chili) in the desert.   _____

STRATEGIC SPELLING: Using the Memory Tricks Strategy

Use memory tricks to help you use homophones correctly. Create homophone sentences for each pair or triplet.

13. chili—chilly _____

14. scent—sent—cent _____

15. their—there—they're _____

Name _____

EXTRA PRACTICE ■ 7

Word List

their	there	they're	wring	ring
chili	chilly	scent	sent	cent
oversees	overseas	patients	patience	cereal
serial	coarse	course	counsel	council

■ **Which Is It?** Use homophones to complete each question-and-answer pair below.

1. Is that new western ___ on TV any good?
2. Yes, except for all the silly ___ commercials.
3. Who is the person who ___ your factories in Asia?
4. Mr. Ray deals with our ___ operations.
5. Would you like a cold drink with your ___?
6. Thanks, but I'm too ___ for that.
7. Why do you have all this ___ wool?
8. I'm taking a ___ in how to make wall hangings.
9. Has the student ___ made a decision yet?
10. No, they're seeking ___ from Ms. Travis first.
11. How many ___ did you see today, Doctor?
12. After about forty, I ran out of ___!
13. Would you ___ out these wet towels?
14. Sure, but let me take my ___ off, first.

■ **Making Inferences** Use homophones to fit the clues below.

15. This helps you pay the bus driver.
16. This is what you did when you mailed a letter.
17. This tells your nose what's for dinner.
18. This word usually makes you think of *where*.
19. This word combines a pronoun and a verb.
20. This tells about belonging to someone.

1. _____
2. _____
3. _____
4. _____
5. _____
6. _____
7. _____
8. _____
9. _____
10. _____
11. _____
12. _____
13. _____
14. _____
15. _____
16. _____
17. _____
18. _____
19. _____
20. _____

Everyday Spelling © Scott Foresman • Addison Wesley

31

7 ■ REVIEW

Word List

their	there	they're	wring	ring
chili	chilly	scent	sent	cent
oversees	overseas	patients	patience	cereal
serial	coarse	course	counsel	council

■ **Making Connections** Write a list word that fits the clues below.

1. This food is peppery hot.
2. A manager does this.
3. Doctors take care of these.
4. This is one penny.
5. Get water out of cloth this way.
6. This is where Africa is.
7. Bloodhounds sniff for this.
8. This describes one type of sandpaper.
9. This might crackle when you add milk.
10. This is done to letters.
11. When you're upset, you run out of this.

■ **Exact Meanings** Write the list word that makes sense in each sentence below.

12. It's a snowy, ___ night outside.
13–14. Of ___ you may have another serving, but I would ___ against it.
15. That newspaper story is a ___, with an episode every Friday.
16. Did someone ___ the doorbell?
17. The ___ voted for a new playground.

■ **Triple Homophones** Complete the paragraph below with three list words that sound alike.

Over __(18)__ are the Puli puppies I told you about, the ones whose hair grows into a mop of coiled ropes. Originally, these intelligent dogs came from Hungary, and __(19)__ great watchdogs for __(20)__ owners.

1. _____
2. _____
3. _____
4. _____
5. _____
6. _____
7. _____
8. _____
9. _____
10. _____
11. _____
12. _____
13. _____
14. _____
15. _____
16. _____
17. _____
18. _____
19. _____
20. _____

CHALLENGE ■ 8

> **Challenge Words**
>
> discipline   indebtedness   monologue   misguided   susceptible

■ Write a Challenge Word to complete each equation.

1. training + obedience = _____

2. wrong + led = _____

3. owing + a state of = _____

4. single + talk = _____

5. sensitive + able = _____

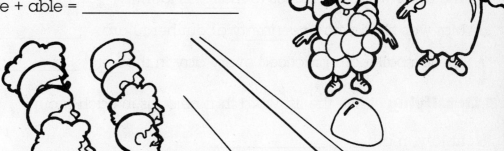

■ People who are known for their talent usually work to apply skill to their talent. Use one or more Challenge Words to write a paragraph about something you do well due to a combination of practice and talent.

_____
_____
_____
_____
_____
_____
_____
_____
_____
_____

8 ■ THINK AND PRACTICE

doubt	fascinate	science	scenic	autumn
column	guilty	league	guardian	disguise

■ **Synonyms** Write a list word that means that same as the underlined word.

1. The mountain drive is <u>beautiful</u>. _____

2. The porch is supported by a tall <u>pillar</u>. _____

3. This book about dolphins will <u>delight</u> you. _____

4. The defendant admitted that he was <u>blamable</u>. _____

5. The actor wore sunglasses to <u>mask</u> his identity. _____

6. Mai was filled with <u>uncertainty</u> about her future. _____

7. The football team practiced every day in the <u>fall</u>. _____

■ **Classifying** Write the list word that belongs in each group.

8. history, math,_____

9. summer, winter,_____

10. team, association,_____

11. parent, baby-sitter,_____

STRATEGIC SPELLING: Seeing Meaning Connections

undoubtedly	doubter	doubtful

12. Write the list word that is related in spelling
and meaning to the words in the box. _____

Complete the sentences with words from the box.

If you were (13)_____ of a fact you read in a newspaper

article, then, (14)_____, you would want to check other

sources. If the other sources confirmed the fact stated in the article, you

would stop being a (15)_____.

Everyday Spelling © Scott Foresman • Addison Wesley

Word List

doubt	fascinate	science	scenic	autumn
column	guilty	league	guardian	disguise
subtle	debt	reminiscent	descend	condemn
solemn	guidance	vague	fatigue	intrigue

■ **Synonyms** Write the list word that means the same as each word below.

1. protector
2. convicted
3. weariness
4. serious
5. camouflage
6. unclear
7. mystery
8. picturesque
9. advice
10. recalling

■ **Base Words** Write the list word that is the base word for each word below.

11. doubtful
12. condemns
13. fascinating
14. scientific
15. columns
16. subtly
17. descendant
18. leagues
19. debtor
20. autumnal

1. _____
2. _____
3. _____
4. _____
5. _____
6. _____
7. _____
8. _____
9. _____
10. _____
11. _____
12. _____
13. _____
14. _____
15. _____
16. _____
17. _____
18. _____
19. _____
20. _____

Everyday Spelling © Scott Foresman • Addison Wesley

8 ■ REVIEW

Word List

doubt	fascinate	science	scenic	autumn
column	guilty	league	guardian	disguise
subtle	debt	reminiscent	descend	condemn
solemn	guidance	vague	fatigue	intrigue

■ **Synonyms** Write a list word that means the same as each word below.

1. gentle   5. conspiracy
2. tire   6. row
3. question   7. hazy
4. spellbind   8. serious

■ **Context Clues** Write the list word that best completes each sentence.

9. The jury found the thief ___ as charged.
10. We decided to take the ___ route along the mountain ridge.
11. Jan's doctor bills put her family in ___.
12. Peter Pan was able to ___ to the stage on an invisible rope.
13. Counselors provide ___.
14. Colorful leaves are the prettiest ___ fashions of all.
15. That perfume is faintly ___ of one my grandmother wore.

■ **Proofreading** Find the misspelled word in each sentence and write it correctly.

16. The judge chose to condenm the criminal's behavior.
17. Jane wants to be the first female player in the leaque.
18. Math and sciance are their best subjects.
19. We recognized Harold despite his disgiuse.
20. Fairy tales are full of gardien angels.

1. _____
2. _____
3. _____
4. _____
5. _____
6. _____
7. _____
8. _____
9. _____
10. _____
11. _____
12. _____
13. _____
14. _____
15. _____
16. _____
17. _____
18. _____
19. _____
20. _____

Everyday Spelling © Scott Foresman • Addison Wesley

Challenge Words

embarrassment   dilemma   unnecessarily
compassionately   accompaniment

■ Use Challenge Words to solve the clues and complete the crossword puzzle.

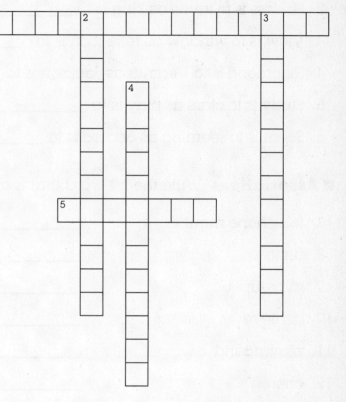

Across
  1. with concern for another
  5. troubling problem

Down
  2. something added
     to the basics
  3. a flustered feeling
  4. needlessly

■ Everyone gets into a difficult situation now and then. Use one or more Challenge Words to write a paragraph about helping someone—or being helped—out of a difficult situation.

_____

_____

_____

_____

_____

_____

Everyday Spelling © Scott Foresman • Addison Wesley

Name _____

9 ■ THINK AND PRACTICE

| connect | command | mirror | accomplish | according |
| allowance | college | address | Mississippi | recess |

■ **Analogies** Write the list word that completes each analogy.

1. Teacher is to school as professor is to _____.

2. Hostess is to invite as king is to _____.

3. View is to window as reflection is to _____.

4. Richmond is to Virginia as Jackson is to _____.

5. Study is to class as play is to _____.

6. Seem is to seeming as accord is to _____.

■ **Associations** Write the list word that is associated with each item.

7. telephone number _____

8. unite _____

9. makeup _____

10. achieve _____

11. playground _____

12. chores _____

13. river _____

STRATEGIC SPELLING: Using the Memory Tricks Strategy
Use memory tricks to help you spell. Choose two list words that are difficult for you. Identify the parts of these words that give you problems. Then create memory tricks for those words. Underline the matching letters in the list words and helpers.

14. _____ _____

_____

15. _____ _____

_____

Everyday Spelling © Scott Foresman • Addison Wesley

Word List

connect	command	mirror	accomplish	according
allowance	college	address	Mississippi	recess
committee	immediate	barricade	interrupt	broccoli
collect	afford	possess	Tennessee	announce

■ **Word Math** Write the list word that completes each equation.

1. green + vitamins + vegetable = ___
2. money + regular + child = ___
3. gate + closed + railroad tracks = ___
4. street + house + number = ___
5. glass + reflect + face = ___
6. group + meeting + discuss = ___
7. microphone + information + speaker = ___
8. study + dorm + degree = ___
9. try + succeed + proud = ___
10. river + Mark Twain + flood = ___

■ **Double Clues** The list words in this lesson all contain double consonants. Use the clues to write list words.

11. Two **m's** give you something right this minute.
12. Two pairs of **s's** means you own it.
13. Two **l's** lets you gather up all your baseball cards.
14. Two **f's** means you have enough money to buy.
15. Two **n's** and two **s's** give you a southern state.
16. Two **r's** is what you do when you break into someone else's conversation.
17. Two **n's** means to join things together.
18. Two **m's** is an order.
19. Two **s's** is a break in the school day.
20. Two **c's** with the word *to* means "based on."

1. _____
2. _____
3. _____
4. _____
5. _____
6. _____
7. _____
8. _____
9. _____
10. _____
11. _____
12. _____
13. _____
14. _____
15. _____
16. _____
17. _____
18. _____
19. _____
20. _____

Everyday Spelling © Scott Foresman • Addison Wesley

9 ■ REVIEW

Word List

connect	command	mirror	accomplish	according
allowance	college	address	Mississippi	recess
committee	immediate	barricade	interrupt	broccoli
collect	afford	possess	Tennessee	announce

■ **Hidden Words** Each word below is hidden in a list word. Write the list word.

1. dress
2. low
3. see
4. and
5. for
6. cord
7. ounce
8. sip
9. up
10. mitt
11. leg
12. media

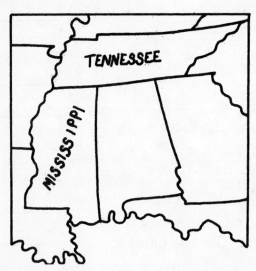

TENNESSEE

MISSISSIPPI

■ **Synonyms in Context** Write a list word that means about the same as the underlined word or words in each sentence.

13. Who's going to <u>gather</u> answer sheets?
14. I didn't <u>associate</u> the two incidents.
15. Did the spies <u>manage to carry off</u> their mission?
16. There was a <u>blockade</u> around the burning house.
17. The children are outside for <u>play</u> period.

■ **Words in Context** Write the list word that could be used to complete each phrase below.

18. ___ on the wall
19. ___ in the salad
20. ___ things

1. _____
2. _____
3. _____
4. _____
5. _____
6. _____
7. _____
8. _____
9. _____
10. _____
11. _____
12. _____
13. _____
14. _____
15. _____
16. _____
17. _____
18. _____
19. _____
20. _____

Everyday Spelling © Scott Foresman • Addison Wesley

Name _____

> ### Challenge Words
>
> | | | |
> |---|---|---|
> | New Year's Eve | millionaire's | millionaires' |
> | roommate's | roommates' | |

■ Complete the following sentences with the correct Challenge Word.

1. The _____ yacht belonged to a group of twelve people.

2. The _____ yacht was her pride and joy.

3. The last night of the year is _____.

4. The _____ bookshelves were things they shared.

5. Her _____ book is on the top shelf.

■ People like to read or think about fantastic adventures. Write an adventure story that uses intriguing details and fantastic events. Use one or more Challenge Words.

_____

_____

_____

_____

_____

_____

_____

_____

_____

_____

_____

_____

_____

10 ■ THINK AND PRACTICE

| it's | let's | that's | we'd | don't |
| there's | coach's | coaches' | man's | men's |

■ **Possessives** Write the correct list word for each sentence.

1. The basketball (coaches', coach's) wife came to every game.

   _____

2. The (men's, man's) locker room was crowded before the swim meet.

   _____

3. That (man's, men's) dog is well-behaved. _____

4. Both (coach's, coaches') suggestions were considered by the players.

   _____

■ **Contractions** Write the contraction for the underlined words
in the sentences.

5. When the movie is over, <u>let us</u> go out for pizza. _____

6. I think <u>there is</u> a monster in the pond. _____

7. Why <u>do not</u> snakes live in Hawaii? _____

8. <u>It is</u> raining, but the sun is shining. _____

9. <u>We had</u> never seen the Grand Canyon before. _____

10. Mom said <u>that is</u> the last piece of pie. _____

11. Do not touch the stove while <u>it is</u> still hot. _____

STRATEGIC SPELLING: Building New Words
Add the contraction for *had* or *would* to the base words. Remember what
you learned.

Base word	**Contraction with -'d**
12. I	_____
13. you	_____
14. he	_____
15. they	_____

Everyday Spelling © Scott Foresman • Addison Wesley

Word List				
it's	let's	that's	we'd	don't
there's	coach's	coaches'	man's	men's
you're	she'd	mustn't	o'clock	guide's
guides'	director's	directors'	city's	cities'

■ **Contractions** Find the words in each sentence that can be made into a contraction. Write the list word contraction.

1. There is a lock on the door.
2. The explosives must not be placed near heat.
3. At noon we had finished our test.
4. I think it is terrible to hurt animals.
5. She would like to invite you for dinner.
6. You are humming while I try to study.
7. The movie begins at seven of the clock.
8. The movie is about to begin, so let us get some popcorn.
9. That is a fine painting of Stu's mother.
10. At our house we do not have snacks before dinner.

■ **Possessives** Write the list word that goes with each phrase below. Belonging to:

11. —the director of the play
12. —one large city
13. —two guides at a state park
14. —the coaches of a professional team
15. —several directors of a company
16. —two adult male persons
17. —more than one city
18. —the guide of a vacation tour
19. —one adult male person
20. —the coach of the volleyball team

1. _____
2. _____
3. _____
4. _____
5. _____
6. _____
7. _____
8. _____
9. _____
10. _____
11. _____
12. _____
13. _____
14. _____
15. _____
16. _____
17. _____
18. _____
19. _____
20. _____

Everyday Spelling © Scott Foresman • Addison Wesley

Name _____

10 ■ REVIEW

■ **Contractions** Write the contraction that contains each word below.

1. she
2. that
3. do
4. let
5. it
6. you
7. clock
8. there
9. we
10. must

1. _____
2. _____
3. _____
4. _____
5. _____
6. _____
7. _____
8. _____
9. _____
10. _____
11. _____
12. _____
13. _____
14. _____
15. _____
16. _____
17. _____
18. _____
19. _____
20. _____

■ **Classifying** Write the list word that belongs in each group.

11. guys', fellows', ___
12. villages', towns', ___
13. trainers', instructors', ___
14. managers', supervisors', ___
15. scouts', trackers', ___

■ **Word Forms** Write the possessive form of each word in parentheses to complete each set of words or phrase.

16. ___ (coach) conference
17. the ___ (guide) binoculars
18. the ___ (city) water system
19. the ___ (man) costume
20. ___ (director) award

Everyday Spelling © Scott Foresman • Addison Wesley

Name _____

Challenge Words

money order   brokenhearted   sweatshirt   turtleneck   health food

---

∎ Put these word pairs together to create the Challenge Words.

1. cash + demand = _____

2. perspiration + garment = _____

3. shattered + organ = _____

4. reptile + body part = _____

5. wellness + nourishment = _____

∎ Have you ever lost something that you cared about? Perhaps a keepsake you treasured was lost. Write a paragraph using one or more Challenge Words to tell about it.

_____

_____

_____

_____

_____

_____

_____

_____

_____

_____

_____

_____

_____

11 ■ THINK AND PRACTICE

myself	themselves	hallway	homeroom	everything
ice cream	locker room	tape recorder	root beer	dead end

■ **Compounds** Match a word from each column to make a list word.
Write the list words.

them   beer   1. _____

home   self   2. _____

tape   selves   3. _____

my   room   4. _____

root   recorder   5. _____

■ **Joining Words** Find two words in each sentence that can be joined to make a list word. Write the word.

6. The cat found a dead bird at the end of the path. _____

7. Lee put cream in the coffee and ice in the tea. _____

8. Every piece of art is a beautiful thing. _____

9. Stuart left his paper at home in his room. _____

10. Do you know the way to the science hall? _____

11. Do you have any room in your locker? _____

12. Maya put a silly thing in every person's desk. _____

STRATEGIC SPELLING: Seeing Meaning Connections

Words with *ice*		
iceberg	ice bag	ice pick

Write the words from the box that fit the clues.

13. a tool for chipping ice _____

14. a floating mass of ice _____

15. a container for applying ice to the body _____

Everyday Spelling © Scott Foresman • Addison Wesley

Word List

myself	themselves	hallway	homeroom	everything
ice cream	locker room	tape recorder	root beer	dead end
teenage	teammate	skateboard	everybody	doughnut
air conditioner	polka dot	roller coaster	ice pack	solar system

■ **Classifying** Write the list word that belongs in each group below.

1. tape deck, video recorder, ___
2. ourselves, yourselves, ___
3. soda pop, ginger ale, ___
4. cupcake, gingersnap, ___
5. Milky Way, full moon, ___
6. classmate, roommate, ___
7. alleyway, pathway, ___
8. Ferris wheel, water slide, ___

■ **Make Them Yourself** Add the missing words to form list words.

9. ___self
10. locker ___
11. home___
12. ___ cream
13. ___board
14. polka ___
15. teen___
16. ___body
17. air ___
18. ___ pack
19. ___thing
20. dead ___

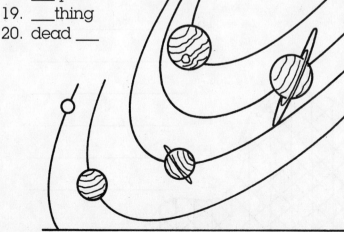

1. _____
2. _____
3. _____
4. _____
5. _____
6. _____
7. _____
8. _____
9. _____
10. _____
11. _____
12. _____
13. _____
14. _____
15. _____
16. _____
17. _____
18. _____
19. _____
20. _____

Name _____

11 ■ REVIEW

Word List

myself	themselves	hallway	homeroom	everything
ice cream	locker room	tape recorder	root beer	dead end
teenage	teammate	skateboard	everybody	doughnut
air conditioner	polka dot	roller coaster	ice pack	solar system

■ **Making Inferences** Write the list word that matches each clue.

1. Earth is one planet in this.
2. There are lots of athletes here.
3. This comes with and without jelly.
4. You'll often find a coat closet here.
5. This makes a trio with *me* and *I*.
6. Useless efforts usually end up here.
7–8. Put these white and brown things together to get a tasty soda.
9. Its power comes from your feet.

■ **Context Clues** Write the list word that completes each sentence.

10. Put an ___ on sprains.
11. The winners should be proud of ___.
12. The ___ broke when the temperature hit 105°F.
13. It seems like ___ is going wrong today.

■ **Word Match** Match the words in each column to make list words. Write the words.

14. every	room
15. tape	body
16. teen	coaster
17. home	dot
18. team	recorder
19. roller	age
20. polka	mate

1. _____
2. _____
3. _____
4. _____
5. _____
6. _____
7. _____
8. _____
9. _____
10. _____
11. _____
12. _____
13. _____
14. _____
15. _____
16. _____
17. _____
18. _____
19. _____
20. _____

Everyday Spelling © Scott Foresman • Addison Wesley

Name _____

Lesson 7				
wring	chili	their	scent	cent

■ **Homophones** Write the correct list word for each sentence.

1. (Wring, Ring) some of the water out of the mop. _____

2. A skunk's (cent, scent) is really strong. _____

3. Do you put beans in your (chilly, chili)? _____

4. When does (there, their) school play begin? _____

5. I spent my last (cent, sent) on stamps. _____

Lesson 8				
doubt	science	autumn	league	guilty

■ **Analogies** Write the list word that completes each analogy.

1. Summer is to winter as spring is to _____.

2. Good is to bad as innocent is to _____.

3. Colleges are to university as teams are to _____.

4. Sure is to certain as uncertainty is to _____.

5. Ball is to sports as microscope is to _____.

Lesson 9				
recess	connect	command	college	Mississippi

■ **Classifying** Write the list word that belongs in each group.

1. join, put together, _____

2. Missouri, Illinois, _____

3. break, rest, _____

4. preschool, junior high, _____

5. order, edict, _____

Everyday Spelling © Scott Foresman • Addison Wesley

12B ■ REVIEW

Lesson 10

coach's	men's	that's	we'd	don't

■ **Seeing Relationships** Write the list word that matches each clue.

1. plural possessive of *man* _____

2. contraction for *that is* _____

3. singular possessive of *coach* _____

4. a word using a contraction for *not* _____

5. a word using a contraction for *had* _____

Lesson 11

hallway	homeroom	ice cream	locker room	dead end

■ **Riddles** Write the list word that answers each riddle.

1. What is used to connect rooms? _____

2. What might be found in a freezer? _____

3. Where might an athlete change clothes? _____

4. Where might a street stop? _____

5. Where might you find a student? _____

Name _____

Challenge Words
malicious   precocious   sensational   vaccination   fictitious

■ Use the Challenge Words listed above to complete these sets of opposites.

1. I thought it was a **true** story, but it turned out to be

   _____.

2. To avoid getting **diseases,** we each got a _____ before
   our trip.

3. Last year's haunted house was **dull,** but this year's will be

   _____.

4. Once he was **kind**; now he is _____.

5. At first, some thought she was **slow to learn** the piano, but she's really

   _____.

■ Imagine you are a reporter, and you have been assigned to tell the real
story of a famous person. Use one or more Challenge Words to set the record
straight.

_____

_____

_____

_____

_____

_____

_____

_____

_____

_____

Name _____

13 ■ THINK AND PRACTICE

social dictionary	precious motion	commercial position	especially population	national question

■ **Synonyms** Write the list word that means the same as each synonym.

1. action _____

2. cherished _____

3. inquire _____

4. location _____

5. particularly _____

6. ad _____

■ **Definitions** Write the list word that fits the definition.

7. a reference book about words _____

8. an advertisement on radio or television _____

9. the number of people who live in a place _____

10. having to do with a country _____

11. having to do with company or companionship _____

12. of great value _____

STRATEGIC SPELLING: Using the Meaning Helpers Strategy

A meaning helper—a shorter word related in spelling and meaning—can help you spell a longer word. For example, thinking of *suggest* will help you remember the **t** in *suggestion*. Write *commercial*, *question*, and *population*. Write a meaning helper below each one and underline the matching letter.

13. _____

_____

14. _____

_____

15. _____

_____

Word List

social	precious	commercial	especially	national
dictionary	motion	position	population	question
artificial	financial	gracious	glacier	suggestion
cautious	mention	fraction	exhaustion	digestion

■ **Analogies** Write a list word to complete each sentence.

1. Note is to symphony as word is to _____.

2. Rock is to mountain as ice is to _____.

3. Ten is to whole number as $\frac{1}{4}$ is to _____.

4. State is to regional as country is to _____.

5. Southwest is to direction as upright is to _____.

6. Certain is to uncertain as answer is to _____.

7. Original is to copy as real is to _____.

8. Sitting is to still as running is to _____.

9. Rash is to foolhardy as wary is to _____.

10. Relate is to relation as populate is to _____.

11. Gravel is to worthless as gold is to _____.

12. School is to educational as bank is to _____.

■ **Spelling Sounds** Write each remaining list word in the column that tells how /**ch**/ or /**sh**/ is spelled.

/**ch**/ spelled *ti*   /**sh**/ spelled *ci*

13. _____   17. _____

14. _____   18. _____

15. _____   19. _____

16. _____   20. _____

Name _____

13 ■ REVIEW

Word List				
social	precious	commercial	especially	national
dictionary	motion	position	population	question
artificial	financial	gracious	glacier	suggestion
cautious	mention	fraction	exhaustion	digestion

■ **Word Forms** Write the list
words that contain the base
words below.

1. suggest
2. finance
3. special
4. digest
5. commerce
6. exhaust

■ **Antonyms** Write the list word
that means the opposite of each
word below.

7. carefree
8. whole
9. omit
10. real
11. answer

■ **Word Addition** Write the list
word that has each meaning and
ending listed below.

12. place + ion
13. people + ion
14. country + al
15. words + definitions + ary
16. ice + mountain + ier
17. get together + al
18. valuable + ous
19. move + ion
20. grace + ous

1. _____
2. _____
3. _____
4. _____
5. _____
6. _____
7. _____
8. _____
9. _____
10. _____
11. _____
12. _____
13. _____
14. _____
15. _____
16. _____
17. _____
18. _____
19. _____
20. _____

Everyday Spelling © Scott Foresman • Addison Wesley

Challenge Words

proceeding	preceding	envelop
envelope	emigrate	immigrate

■ Write a Challenge Word to match each definition.

1. to wrap or cover _____

2. leave one's country to settle in another _____

3. going on after having stopped _____

4. paper cover for mailing _____

5. coming before _____

6. come into a country to live _____

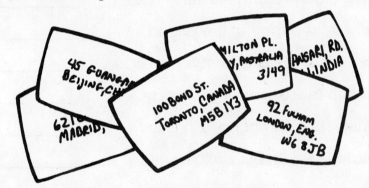

■ Talk to family members and friends to find someone who came to this country from another country. Then use Challenge Words to write a paragraph about the person and his or her native land.

_____

_____

_____

_____

_____

_____

_____

_____

Name _____

14 ■ THINK AND PRACTICE

| since | sense | choose | chose | finally |
| finely | except | accept | beside | besides |

■ Making Connections Write the list word that matches each clue.

1. How you might chop onions for a recipe   _____

2. The opposite of *reject*   _____

3. What you do when you have two options   _____

4. Sight, smell, touch, taste, or sound   _____

■ Word Choice Write the correct list word for each sentence.

5. Everyone ate the eggplant (except, accept) Tim.   _____

6. The concert was (finely, finally) over.   _____

7. Sue (choose, chose) a puppy at the pound.   _____

8. No one (beside, besides) Carlo knows the code.   _____

9. I haven't seen him (since, sense) yesterday.   _____

10. Tina put in (finely, finally) chopped parsley.   _____

11. Olivia sat (besides, beside) her brother.   _____

STRATEGIC SPELLING: Seeing Meaning Connections
Complete each sentence with a word from the box.

| Words with *accept* | | | |
| acceptance | acceptable | acceptably | unacceptable |

12. Student: "I hope my paper is _____."

13. Teacher: "No, this messy work is _____."

14. Student: "How can I gain your _____?"

15. Teacher: "Turn in an _____ written paper."

Everyday Spelling © Scott Foresman • Addison Wesley

Name _____

Word List

since	sense	choose	chose	finally
finely	except	accept	beside	besides
recent	resent	access	excess	later
latter	metal	medal	personal	personnel

■ **Word Math** Write a list word to complete each equation.

1. iron + copper + lead =
2. winner + ceremony + prize =
3. company + employee + hire =
4. private + individual + shy =
5. food + too much + stomachache =
6. ramp + wheelchair + openness =
7. insult + response + anger =
8. yesterday + new + fresh =

■ **Which Is It?** Use a list word to complete each sentence below.

9. Didn't you ___ a sweater already?
10. Yes, I ___ this wool sweater.
11. I've finished all my assignments ___ for geography.
12. Maybe Mr. Singh will ___ your homework late.
13. Lin has not practiced her flute ___ Wednesday.
14. That's strange, she usually has better ___ than that.
15. Of the two movies I saw, I preferred the ___.
16. I hope I'll get a chance to see it ___.
17. Do you want to sit ___ me at the awards dinner?
18. Yes, and how many people are coming ___ us?
19. The tomatoes have to be chopped more ___ than that.
20. Yes, I think I've ___ learned how to do it!

1. _____
2. _____
3. _____
4. _____
5. _____
6. _____
7. _____
8. _____
9. _____
10. _____
11. _____
12. _____
13. _____
14. _____
15. _____
16. _____
17. _____
18. _____
19. _____
20. _____

Everyday Spelling © Scott Foresman • Addison Wesley

57

14 ■ REVIEW

Word List

since	sense	choose	chose	finally
finely	except	accept	beside	besides
recent	resent	access	excess	later
latter	metal	medal	personal	personnel

■ **Synonyms** Write the list word that means the same as the words in each group below.

1. private, individual, ___
2. feeling, awareness, ___
3. approve of, agree to, ___
4. next to, near, ___
5. pick, select, ___
6. current, new, ___
7. overflow, extra, ___
8. award, prize, ___
9. at last, eventually, ___
10. staff, employees, ___

■ **Definitions** Write the list words that mean the same as the underlined words.

11. The class will begin <u>after the usual time</u>.
12. The game will stop until another time <u>because</u> it is raining.
13. John likes all candy flavors <u>but</u> licorice.
14. <u>Other than</u> these, I think I've read all the books.
15. Lee will <u>take offense</u> at any interference.
16. Randy <u>picked</u> the black shoes.
17. The <u>opening</u> to the cave was on the north side of the mountain.

■ **Seeing Relationships** Write a list word that fits the clues below.

18. This describes the second of two things.
19. This is shiny and cold.
20. Very small pieces have been chopped this way.

1. _____
2. _____
3. _____
4. _____
5. _____
6. _____
7. _____
8. _____
9. _____
10. _____
11. _____
12. _____
13. _____
14. _____
15. _____
16. _____
17. _____
18. _____
19. _____
20. _____

Everyday Spelling © Scott Foresman • Addison Wesley

Challenge Words
exquisite   mischievous   refrigerator   pastime   anxious

■ Use Challenge Words to fill in the blanks in the following conversation.

"That crystal vase is _____! I am so _____ that it might fall and break!"

"I'll put it out of reach on the _____."

"I'm sure my _____ cat will jump up there and knock the vase down!"

"Calm down! I think worrying is your favorite _____."

■ Sometimes people create conversations to practice what to say at a party or on a job interview. Use one or more Challenge Words to write a practice interview for a job.

_____

_____

_____

_____

_____

_____

_____

_____

Everyday Spelling © Scott Foresman • Addison Wesley

15 ■ THINK AND PRACTICE

| similar | doesn't | experience | forward | exactly |
| partner | drawer | expensive | develop | familiar |

■ **Drawing Conclusions** Write the list word that answers each question.

1. Where might you keep your socks? _____

2. What can help you get a job? _____

3. Who works with you? _____

4. What do you do to a roll of film to get pictures? _____

5. How should you do measurements? _____

6. What word would you use to describe synonyms? _____

■ **Antonyms** Write the list word that completes each phrase.

7. not cheap, but _____

8. not strange, but _____

9. not backward, but _____

10. not different, but _____

11. not does, but _____

STRATEGIC SPELLING: Using the Memory Tricks Strategy

Use memory tricks to help you spell. Create memory tricks using the list words and helpers below. Underline the matching letters.

12. exactly—act _____

   _____

13. drawer—draw _____

   _____

14. doesn't—doe _____

   _____

15. forward—for _____

   _____

Everyday Spelling © Scott Foresman • Addison Wesley

Word List

similar	doesn't	experience	forward	exactly
partner	drawer	expensive	develop	familiar
pigeon	tickling	penalty	frustrated	athletic
celebration	circling	helicopter	trembling	sparkling

■ **Classifying** Write the list word that belongs in each group below.

1. costly, high priced, ___
2. backward, sideways, ___
3. dove, crow, ___
4. plane, blimp, ___
5. co-worker, helper, ___
6. vigorous, acrobatic, ___
7. shaking, shuddering, ___
8. party, reception, ___
9. fine, punishment, ___
10. don't, won't, ___
11. angry, dissatisfied, ___

1. _____
2. _____
3. _____
4. _____
5. _____
6. _____
7. _____
8. _____
9. _____
10. _____
11. _____

■ **Puzzle** Complete each list word in the blanks below. The circled letters will give you the answer to the riddle.

12. ___ **x** ___ (○) ___ ___ ___
13. ___ (○) ___ **m** ___ ___ ___ ___
14. ___ ___ ___ **w** ___ (○) ___
15. ___ ___ **p** ___ ___ ___ ___ (○) ___
16. ___ ___ ___ ___ (○) ___ **p** ___
17. **f** ___ ___ (○) ___ ___ ___ ___ ___
18. ___ ___ ___ **k** ___ (○) ___
19. ___ **p** ___ ___ ___ ___ (○)

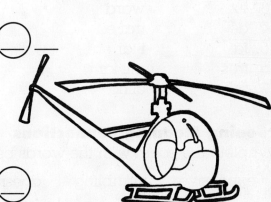

What does the captain say your plane is doing if the airport is crowded?

20. ___ ___ ___ ___ ___ ___ ___ ___

Name _____

Word List

similar	doesn't	experience	forward	exactly
partner	drawer	expensive	develop	familiar
pigeon	tickling	penalty	frustrated	athletic
celebration	circling	helicopter	trembling	sparkling

■ **Drawing Conclusions** Write the list word that answers each question.

1. What vehicle has a pinwheel top?
2. What's funny that you want to stop immediately?
3. What coos and carries a message?
4. Who do police officers turn to for help?
5. How do white teeth look?
6. What does an offensive foul require?
7. What often requires a special cake?
8. What keeps your socks out of sight?
9. What kind of contest is just between sports?
10. What do employers often look for?

■ **Combining Syllables** Combine each syllable in the first column with a syllable or syllables from the second column to make a list word.

11. cir	act ly
12. for	vel op
13. ex	ward
14. de	trat ed
15. fa	i lar
16. frus	mil iar
17. sim	cling

■ **Seeing Meaning Connections**
Complete the poem with the words below.

    expensive   trembling   doesn't

It (18) take an expert,
To say with voice a' (19) ,
That beautiful jewels are (20) ,
And payments, never-ending.

1. _____
2. _____
3. _____
4. _____
5. _____
6. _____
7. _____
8. _____
9. _____
10. _____
11. _____
12. _____
13. _____
14. _____
15. _____
16. _____
17. _____
18. _____
19. _____
20. _____

Challenge Words		
mosquitoes	desperadoes	flamingos
wharves	bailiffs	

■ Answer the following questions using Challenge Words.

1. Which would you see in an Old West movie? _____

2. Which insects would you find in hot, steamy weather? _____

3. Which would you hope to see when pleasure boating in Florida?

_____

4. Which would you hope to see when docking a boat? _____

5. Which work in a courtroom? _____

■ Folktales and lore about the Old West are an important part of our culture. Write a paragraph describing your favorite story about the Old West—or make up an outline for a story of your own.

_____

_____

_____

_____

_____

_____

_____

16 ■ THINK AND PRACTICE

scarfs	staffs	shelves	wolves	ourselves
solos	stereos	volcanoes	quizzes	pants

■ **Classifying** Write the list word that belongs in each group.

1. televisions, radios, _____

2. quartets, duets, _____

3. closets, drawers, _____

4. homework, exams, _____

■ **Context** Write the list word that completes each sentence.

5. Alicia wears colorful _____ that match her clothes.

6. In the mountains, you can hear _____ howling at night.

7. We laughed at _____ for forgetting the tickets.

8. The library and teaching _____ had a party.

9. Ivan learned how to iron a pair of _____.

10. Mauna Loa is one of Hawaii's most famous _____.

11. Mr. Alvarez's _____ are filled with books on every subject.

STRATEGIC SPELLING: Building New Words
Add either **-s** or **-es** to each word. If you're not sure how to spell the plural, look in your Spelling Dictionary.

12. belief _____

13. elf _____

14. echo _____

15. piano _____

Everyday Spelling © Scott Foresman • Addison Wesley

Word List

scarfs	staffs	shelves	wolves	ourselves
solos	stereos	volcanoes	quizzes	pants
sheriffs	reefs	chiefs	knives	thieves
studios	dominoes	buffaloes	scissors	measles

■ Double Plurals Write list words to complete the sentences.

1. Dad painted the cupboards and _____ in the kitchen.

2. The musical program contained several duets and _____.

3. Sara likes to wear bright hats and _____.

4. It took several deputies and _____ to catch the outlaws.

5. Many shipwrecks have been caused by dangerous _____.

6. Grandma had mumps and _____ as a child.

7. The land was devastated by earthquakes and _____.

8. This book describes how dogs and _____ are different.

9. Jay took all his shirts and _____ to the cleaners.

10. They have a sale on cassette players and _____.

11. Horses and _____ were important to the Plains Indians.

12. Crayons and _____ are supplies that you use in school.

■ Plurals Write the list word that is the plural form of each word below.

13. studio _____   17. thief _____

14. chief _____   18. domino _____

15. knife _____   19. ourself _____

16. staff _____   20. quiz _____

Everyday Spelling © Scott Foresman • Addison Wesley

Name _____

16 ■ REVIEW

Word List

scarfs	staffs	shelves	wolves	ourselves
solos	stereos	volcanoes	quizzes	pants
sheriffs	reefs	chiefs	knives	thieves
studios	dominoes	buffaloes	scissors	measles

■ **Context Clues** Add **-s** or **-es** to each word in parentheses to form a list word that completes each sentence.

1. Today, (buffalo) are raised on farms.
2. We could hear the (wolf) howling nearby.
3. Let's scuba-dive off the coral (reef).
4. The (thief) broke in through the door.
5. The art (studio) will be near the river.
6. Put the (knife) on the table.
7. The (staff) of workers are being added to.
8. In the Old West, the (sheriff) once reigned.
9. The (stereo) will go on sale Friday.
10. The (volcano) erupted with great force.
11. The concert will end after the final (solo).

■ **Rhymes** Write the list word that makes sense in the verse.

12. To the midwinter dance,
    Wear your wool ___ .
13. Help yourselves
    To the pies on the ___ .
14. Scholarly whizzes
    Ace all their ___ .
15. Go to your easels
    And draw dots like ___.
16. We don't need elves.
    We'll do it ___ .
17. A block pattern grows
    As you play ___ .

■ **Synonyms** Write the list word that means the same as each word below.

18. shears   20. leaders
19. neckwear

1. _____
2. _____
3. _____
4. _____
5. _____
6. _____
7. _____
8. _____
9. _____
10. _____
11. _____
12. _____
13. _____
14. _____
15. _____
16. _____
17. _____
18. _____
19. _____
20. _____

Everyday Spelling © Scott Foresman • Addison Wesley

66

Challenge Words

haste	hasten	heir
inherit	harmony	harmonious

■ Complete the following sentences using the correct form of the Challenge Words.

HURRY

You make _____.

You _____ to the store.

RELATIONSHIPS

You can create _____.

You can spend a _____ evening with friends.

FAMILY

If your parents write a will, you are an _____.

You can _____ wealth or objects.

■ Doing things faster isn't always better. Remember the saying "haste makes waste"? Write a paragraph about a time that proved that saying to be true. Use one or more Challenge Words.

_____

_____

_____

_____

_____

_____

_____

_____

_____

17 ■ THINK AND PRACTICE

human	humane	clean	cleanse	nature
natural	major	majority	poem	poetic

■ **Word Relationships** Write the list word that matches each clue.
Then write the list word that is related to it.

a written work in verse 1. _____ 2. _____

greater in importance 3. _____ 4. _____

not dirty 5. _____ 6. _____

■ **Related Pairs** To complete each sentence, write two list words
that are related.

7. Be sure to _____ the cut on your finger with

   _____ water.

8. Every _____ being should be _____

   to animals.

9. You may not think you are _____, but you can write

   a good _____.

10. Aaron felt most _____ when he was outdoors enjoying

    _____.

11. This _____ has the most _____ description

    of daffodils that I have ever read.

12. It is only _____ for animals such as lions to live

    in _____.

STRATEGIC SPELLING: Seeing Meaning Connections

Write the word from the box that completes each phrase.
Use a dictionary if you need help.

13. represent as human _____

14. mankind _____

15. a person promoting social reform _____

humanity
humanitarian
humanize

Everyday Spelling © Scott Foresman • Addison Wesley

Name _____

Word List

human	humane	clean	cleanse	nature
natural	major	majority	poem	poetic
equal	equation	unite	unity	bomb
bombard	muscle	muscular	resign	resignation

■ **Adding Endings** Write the list word that is formed when you add each base word and ending below.

1. resign + ation
2. nature + al
3. unite + y
4. major + ity
5. equate + ion
6. muscle + ar
7. poet + ic
8. human + e

$2+2=4$
$4+4=8$
$8+8=16$

$2 \times 2=4$
$4 \times 4=16$
$8 \times 8=64$

1. _____
2. _____
3. _____
4. _____
5. _____
6. _____
7. _____
8. _____

■ **Variety** Write each remaining list word on the line under its description. Which words have:

—the long **e** sound?

9. _____

10. _____

—the **z** sound spelled *s*?

11. _____

12. _____

—the long **u** sound?

13. _____

14. _____

—a silent letter?

15. _____

16. _____

—the **ər** sound?

17. _____

18. _____

—the long **o** sound?

19. _____

—the short **o** sound?

20. _____

17 ■ REVIEW

Word List

human	humane	clean	cleanse	nature
natural	major	majority	poem	poetic
equal	equation	unite	unity	bomb
bombard	muscle	muscular	resign	resignation

■ **Classifying** Write the list word that belongs in each group.

1. bone, tendon, ___
2. spotless, immaculate, ___
3. unspoiled, unaffected, ___
4. kind, charitable, ___
5. important, large, ___
6. retirement, termination, ___
7. grenade, missile, ___
8. join, combine, ___
9. rhythmic, rhyming, ___
10. same, identical, ___

■ **Complete a Poem** Write list words to complete the poem.

The minority—no, the (11)—yes,
Answered the math (12) with a guess.
To (13) my mind of number thought,
I wrote a verse of a (14) on the spot.
It goes: A (15) being is what I am.
It's not in my (16) to like to cram.
So please slow down when things get hard,
With numbers, please do not (17).

■ **Antonyms** Write the list word that means the opposite of each word below.

18. division
19. puny
20. join

1. _____
2. _____
3. _____
4. _____
5. _____
6. _____
7. _____
8. _____
9. _____
10. _____
11. _____
12. _____
13. _____
14. _____
15. _____
16. _____
17. _____
18. _____
19. _____
20. _____

Everyday Spelling © Scott Foresman • Addison Wesley

Name _____

Lesson 13

precious	commercial	dictionary	question	population

■ **Classifying** Write the list word that belongs in each group.

1. advertisement, message, _____

2. encyclopedia, almanac, _____

3. people, inhabitants, _____

4. valuable, expensive, _____

5. inquiry, request, _____

Lesson 14

choose	finely	except	beside	sense

■ **Context** Write the list word that completes each sentence.

1. When you mince parsley, you chop it _____.

2. Remember to use common _____ in an emergency.

3. We stood quietly _____ the crib.

4. Which sweater did you _____?

5. Everyone _____ Matt went to the game.

Lesson 15

similar	experience	exactly	partner	familiar

■ **Definitions** Write the list word that means the same as the underlined word or words.

1. My person who shares and I drew a map. _____

2. Do you have any practice working with pets? _____

3. That music sounds well-known to me. _____

4. The book costs precisely seven dollars. _____

5. This building looks very much the same
   to that one. _____

Name _____

18B ■ REVIEW

Lesson 16

| wolves | volcanoes | staffs | solos | pants |

■ **Word Forms** Write the list word that is the plural form of each word.

1. volcano   _____

2. pants   _____

3. solo   _____

4. wolf   _____

5. staff   _____

Lesson 17

| humane | clean | nature | majority | poetic |

■ **Seeing Relationships** Write the list word that matches each clue.

1. If you write a <u>poem</u>, then you are this.   _____

2. If something is all <u>natural</u>, then it comes from this.   _____

3. A <u>human</u> who is kind to animals is said to be this.   _____

4. If you <u>cleanse</u> something, then it will be this.   _____

5. To make a <u>major</u> change, sometimes this
is needed.   _____

Everyday Spelling © Scott Foresman • Addison Wesley

Challenge Words

pessimism   prominent   controversy   suspicious   porpoise

■ Use Challenge Words to complete the relationships described below.

_____ is to optimism as bad news is to good news.

_____ is to trusting as approval is to disapproval.

_____ is to whale as chimpanzee is to ape.

_____ is to consensus as disagreement is to agreement.

_____ is to noticeable as new is to unused.

■ Zoos are the setting for exciting programs to save, breed, and restore the health of animals. Use one or more Challenge Words to write a paragraph of zoo news.

_____

_____

_____

_____

_____

_____

_____

_____

_____

_____

_____

_____

_____

19 ■ THINK AND PRACTICE

different	register	carnival	variety	atmosphere
favorite	pattern	understand	sentence	instance

■ **Synonyms** Write a list word that means the same as the underlined word.

1. Mario won a prize at the fair.   _____

2. Tara did not comprehend the question.   _____

3. The wallpaper had a flowered design.   _____

4. Macaroni is Keesha's preferred food.   _____

5. The salad had an interesting mixture of fruits.   _____

■ **Definitions** Write the list word that fits each definition.

6. a group of words that states
   a complete thought   _____

7. not the same as   _____

8. an example or illustration   _____

9. one that is liked best   _____

10. the air surrounding the earth   _____

11. to enroll or sign up   _____

STRATEGIC SPELLING: Using the Divide and Conquer Strategy

Sometimes it helps to study long words piece by piece. Write four list words that are hard for you. Draw lines between the syllables. Then study the words syllable by syllable. Check the Spelling Dictionary if you need help.

12. _____   14. _____

13. _____   15. _____

Everyday Spelling © Scott Foresman • Addison Wesley

Word List

different	register	carnival	variety	atmosphere
favorite	pattern	understand	sentence	instance
elegant	aquarium	communicate	gasoline	factory
definite	Chicago	heavily	garage	illustrate

■ **Pronunciations** Write a list word for each pronunciation.

1. (fak′tər ē)
2. (fā′vər it)
3. (def′ə nit)
4. (dif′ər ənt)
5. (gə räzh′)
6. (gas′ə lēn′)
7. (shə kô′gō)
8. (kär′nə vəl)
9. (il′ə strāt)
10. (in′stəns)
11. (hev′ə lē)
12. (və rī ′ə tē)

■ **Base Words** Write the list word that is the base word for each word below.

13. sentences
14. unregistered
15. misunderstanding
16. elegantly
17. communicable
18. aquariums
19. atmospheric
20. patterning

1. _____
2. _____
3. _____
4. _____
5. _____
6. _____
7. _____
8. _____
9. _____
10. _____
11. _____
12. _____
13. _____
14. _____
15. _____
16. _____
17. _____
18. _____
19. _____
20. _____

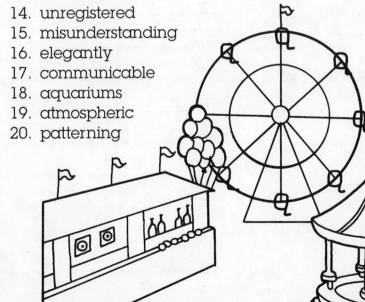

Everyday Spelling © Scott Foresman • Addison Wesley

19 ■ REVIEW

Word List

different	register	carnival	variety	atmosphere
favorite	pattern	understand	sentence	instance
elegant	aquarium	communicate	gasoline	factory
definite	Chicago	heavily	garage	illustrate

■ **Word Math** Answer each problem with a list word.

1. machines + manufacture = ___
2. cotton candy + rides + people = ___
3. station + tank + hose = ___
4. fish + water + tank = ___
5. noun + verb + period = ___
6. cars + tools + service people = ___
7. air + moisture + heat = ___

■ **Analogies** Write the list word that completes each analogy.

8. Skip is to lightly as plod is to ___.
9. St. Louis is to Missouri as ___ is to Illinois.
10. Insecure is to doubtful as assured is to ___.
11. Attend is to enroll as to vote is to ___.
12. Pencil is to write as brush is to ___.
13. Limousine is to luxurious as gown is to ___.
14. Drawing is to outline as sew is to ___.
15. Liver is to dreaded as chocolate is to ___.

■ **Context Clues** Write the list word that completes each sentence.

16. Do you ___ fractions?
17. There wasn't a single ___ of tardiness the whole week.
18. Try to ___ your differences calmly.
19. There's a ___ of fruits to pick from.
20. Take a ___ approach if this one doesn't work.

1. _____
2. _____
3. _____
4. _____
5. _____
6. _____
7. _____
8. _____
9. _____
10. _____
11. _____
12. _____
13. _____
14. _____
15. _____
16. _____
17. _____
18. _____
19. _____
20. _____

Everyday Spelling © Scott Foresman • Addison Wesley

Challenge Words

enlighten   toboggan   pummel   disentangle   denominator

■ Use Challenge Words to solve the clues below. Then use the combined clues to spell vertically the word meaning "lower part of a fraction."

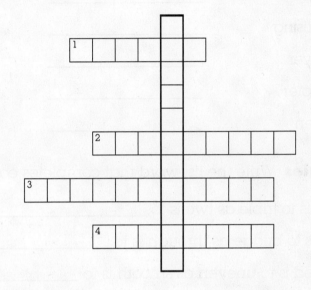

1. beat with fists
2. instruct
3. sort out
4. long, narrow sled

■ Skating, sledding, and tobogganing are winter sports. Choose a sport and write a paragraph that persuades a friend to participate in your sport. Use one or more Challenge Words.

_____

_____

_____

_____

_____

_____

_____

_____

Everyday Spelling © Scott Foresman • Addison Wesley

20 ■ THINK AND PRACTICE

| slogan | citizen | forgotten | propeller | collector |
| level | tunnel | double | single | example |

■ **Associations** Write the list word that is related to each item.

1. one _____

2. instance _____

3. advertising _____

4. taxpayer _____

5. helicopter _____

6. forgiven _____

■ **Analogies** Write the list word that completes each analogy.

7. Three is to triple as two is to _____.

8. Over is to bridge as through is to _____.

9. Crooked is to uneven as smooth is to _____.

10. Perform is to performer as collect is to _____.

11. Loved is to hated as remembered is to _____.

STRATEGIC SPELLING: Seeing Meaning Connections

Write the words from the box that fit the definitions.

Words related to *collect*	
collector	collection
collectible	recollect

12. to remember _____

13. an object that is gathered in a group as a hobby _____

14. one who accumulates objects for study or as a hobby _____

15. a group of objects _____

Everyday Spelling © Scott Foresman • Addison Wesley

Word List

slogan	citizen	forgotten	propeller	collector
level	tunnel	double	single	example
urban	orphan	kindergarten	encounter	conquer
appetizer	dishonor	tractor	easel	recycle

■ **Analogies** Use a list word to complete each sentence below.

1. Teenager is to high school as child is to ___.
2. Garage is to car as barn is to ___.
3. Water is to pipe as cars are to ___.
4. Club is to member as nation is to ___.
5. Observe is to examine as defeat is to ___.
6. Farm is to rural as factory is to ___.
7. Mountain is to uneven as plateau is to ___.
8. Inspect is to inspector as collect is to ___.
9. Writer is to notebook as painter is to ___.
10. Inform is to news story as persuade is to ___.

■ **Making Inferences** Write a list word to match each clue.

11. This gets you to first base.
12. A puppy without a mother or father is this.
13. This is something like a model.
14. We do this to ourselves when we betray a friend.
15. This is a fancy word for a meeting.
16. You might have done this when you weren't reminded.
17. This gets you to second base.
18. Too much of this spoils your dinner.
19. This is not needed by a jet plane.
20. Do this to help conserve the earth's resources.

1. _____
2. _____
3. _____
4. _____
5. _____
6. _____
7. _____
8. _____
9. _____
10. _____
11. _____
12. _____
13. _____
14. _____
15. _____
16. _____
17. _____
18. _____
19. _____
20. _____

Everyday Spelling © Scott Foresman • Addison Wesley

20 ■ REVIEW

Word List

slogan	citizen	forgotten	propeller	collector
level	tunnel	double	single	example
urban	orphan	kindergarten	encounter	conquer
appetizer	dishonor	tractor	easel	recycle

■ **Complete a Poem** Complete the poem with list words.

I liked drawing on the _(1)_ .
When I was five in _(2)_ ,
I did it every _(3)_ day.
I have remembered, not _(4)_ .
Now I _(5)_ through the dirt
To _(6)_ foes down deep.
For I'm an avid rock _(7)_ .
The best of rocks I keep.

1. _____
2. _____
3. _____
4. _____
5. _____
6. _____
7. _____

■ **Context Clues** Write the list word that completes each sentence.

8. The ___ for the ad is funny.
9. The ___ on the chalkboard helped the class do the problem.
10. We're helping to ___ waste materials.
11. The farmer climbed onto the ___.
12. A ___ has many rights, but also many responsibilities.
13. The airplane's ___ broke loose from the motor.
14. The twins' criminal life brought ___ to their family.
15. Many rivers around ___ areas are polluted.
16. The ___ was adopted immediately.

8. _____
9. _____
10. _____
11. _____
12. _____
13. _____
14. _____
15. _____
16. _____
17. _____
18. _____
19. _____
20. _____

■ **Classifying** Write the list word that belongs in each group.

17. twice, twofold, ___
18. soup, salad, ___
19. even, straight, ___
20. meet, confront, ___

Everyday Spelling © Scott Foresman • Addison Wesley

Challenge Words

informative   remorseful   trustworthy   furthermore   observable

---

■ Find the Challenge Word that fits the clue. Then write a sentence using that word.

1. full of facts _____

2. in addition _____

3. visible _____

4. reliable _____

5. sorry for _____

■ Imagine that someone is on trial for a crime he or she did not commit. You are the lawyer for the defense. Use one or more Challenge Words to introduce your client to the jury.

_____

_____

_____

_____

_____

_____

_____

_____

_____

_____

_____

_____

Everyday Spelling © Scott Foresman • Addison Wesley

21 ■ THINK AND PRACTICE

| report | order | explore | ignore | expert |
| service | research | worth | worst | disturb |

■ **Base Words** Write the list word that is the base word
of each word.

1. serviceable   _____

2. inexpert   _____

3. disturbance   _____

4. exploratory   _____

5. disorder   _____

■ **Context** Write the list word that is missing from
each person's statement.

6. Scientist: "I have done _____ on earthquakes."

7. Jeweler: "Your diamond ring is _____ thousands
of dollars."

8. Dentist: "Don't _____ a pain in your tooth."

9. Newscaster: "Stay tuned for a special _____."

10. Meteorologist: "This is the _____ flooding
in thirty years."

STRATEGIC SPELLING: Building New Words

Complete the chart by adding **-ed** and **-ing** to each
of these words: *report, ignore, order, research, explore.*

Add -ed	Add -ing
11. _____	_____
12. _____	_____
13. _____	_____
14. _____	_____
15. _____	_____

Everyday Spelling © Scott Foresman • Addison Wesley

Name _____

Word List

report	order	explore	ignore	expert
service	research	worth	worst	disturb
sword	forty	enormous	therefore	determine
permanent	earning	thorough	attorney	purchase

■ **Making Inferences** Write the list word that each sentence makes you think of.

1. Juan has two twenty-dollar bills.
2. That was the most awful TV show I've ever seen.
3. Are they going to sue the company?
4. Ahmed knows more about the solar system than anyone.
5. Are you going to buy a new car this year?
6. This medieval weapon is still in good condition.
7. The structure has been made to last a long time.
8. Why do you always interrupt me when I'm practicing?
9. Kim plans to study rain forest plants and animals.
10. The monster in the film filled the screen.

1. _____
2. _____
3. _____
4. _____
5. _____
6. _____
7. _____
8. _____
9. _____
10. _____

■ **How Is It Spelled?** Write each remaining list word in the column that tells how it is spelled.

ėr sound spelled *er*

11. _____

12. _____

ėr sound spelled *or*

13. _____

14. _____

ėr sound spelled *ear*

15. _____

ôr sound spelled *or*

16. _____

17. _____

ôr sound spelled *ore*

18. _____

19. _____

20. _____

21 ■ REVIEW

Word List

report	order	explore	ignore	expert
service	research	worth	worst	disturb
sword	forty	enormous	therefore	determine
permanent	earning	thorough	attorney	purchase

■ **Antonyms** Write the list word that completes each phrase.

1. not the *best*, but the ___
2. not *see to*, but ___
3. not *temporary*, but ___
4. not *sell*, but ___
5. not *amateur*, but ___
6. not *tiny*, but ___
7. not *spending*, but ___
8. not *partial*, but ___

■ **Classifying** Write the list word that belongs in each group.

9. judge, bailiff, ___
10. four, fourteen, ___
11. demand, command, ___
12. talk, presentation, ___
13. bother, trouble, ___
14. seek, quest, ___
15. so, after all, ___
16. decide, conclude, ___
17. lance, helmet, ___

■ **Synonyms in Context** Write a list word that means about the same as the underlined word or words in each sentence.

18. He did me the <u>favor</u> of raking the leaves.
19. The antiques' <u>value</u> is unknown.
20. Look up magazine articles as part of your <u>investigation</u>.

1. _____
2. _____
3. _____
4. _____
5. _____
6. _____
7. _____
8. _____
9. _____
10. _____
11. _____
12. _____
13. _____
14. _____
15. _____
16. _____
17. _____
18. _____
19. _____
20. _____

Everyday Spelling © Scott Foresman • Addison Wesley

Name _____

Challenge Words

administration   investigation   exhibition   prescription   cancellation

---

■ Write the Challenge Word by adding the suffix.

1. administer _____

2. investigate _____

3. exhibit _____

4. prescribe _____

5. cancel _____

■ Imagine you are an art critic attending a big exhibition. Use one or more Challenge Words to write your review about the art gallery.

_____

_____

_____

_____

_____

_____

_____

_____

Name _____

22 ■ THINK AND PRACTICE

| relaxation | exploration | occupation | destination | infection |
| collection | reaction | situation | television | convention |

■ **Making Connections** Write the list word that tells what each person has.

1. collector _____

2. video viewer _____

3. employee _____

4. traveler _____

5. patient _____

■ **Context Clues** Add a suffix to each word in parentheses to form a list word to complete each sentence.

6. The beach is a good place for (relax). _____

7. What was Tricia's (react) to the surprise party? _____

8. They have a (convene) every four years. _____

9. Marine biologists perform underwater (explore). _____

10. Joe was in the hospital with a serious (infect). _____

11. How would you handle the (situate)? _____

STRATEGIC SPELLING: Building New Words

Add the suffix **-tion** to the following base words: *deceive, reduce, resolve, assume.* Use your Spelling Dictionary if you need help.

12. _____   14. _____

13. _____   15. _____

Everyday Spelling © Scott Foresman • Addison Wesley

Word List

relaxation	exploration	occupation	destination	infection
collection	reaction	situation	television	convention
orientation	recommendation	determination	generation	reflection
destruction	attention	deduction	reception	solution

■ **Words in Context** Write a list word to complete each person's statement below.

1. Mother: "The people in your grandfather's ___ lived through the Depression."
2. Math Teacher: "What ___ did you get to that problem?"
3. Museum Guide: "This is a fine ___ of Egyptian art."
4. Clerk: "With a price ___ of 10%, your charge will be $7.56."
5. Engineer: "This new ___ set is computer controlled."
6. City Official: "The ___ caused by the storm was extensive."
7. Astronomer: "The ___ of the solar system has told much about Earth."
8. Police Officer: "A ___ is never hopeless."
9. Doctor: "Use this cream to avoid ___."
10. Announcer: "May I have your ___, please!"
11. Counselor: "We will have middle school ___ all week."
12. Job Interviewer: "What was your last ___?"

■ **Riddles** Write the list word that matches each clue.

13. a warm bath
14. a full meeting hall
15. someone jumping in fright
16. gritted teeth
17. a lake with a smooth surface
18. a road map
19. the picture on a TV set
20. a letter full of praise

1. _____
2. _____
3. _____
4. _____
5. _____
6. _____
7. _____
8. _____
9. _____
10. _____
11. _____
12. _____
13. _____
14. _____
15. _____
16. _____
17. _____
18. _____
19. _____
20. _____

Everyday Spelling © Scott Foresman • Addison Wesley

22 ■ REVIEW

Word List

relaxation	exploration	occupation	destination	infection
collection	reaction	situation	television	convention
orientation	recommendation	determination	generation	reflection
destruction	attention	deduction	reception	solution

■ **Associations** Write the list word that is associated with each item below.

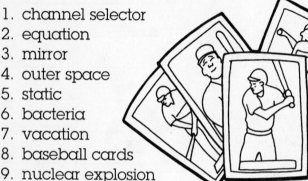

1. channel selector
2. equation
3. mirror
4. outer space
5. static
6. bacteria
7. vacation
8. baseball cards
9. nuclear explosion
10. Sherlock Holmes
11. political party

■ **Word Forms** Write the list word that contains the base word below.

12. recommend
13. orient
14. react

■ **Synonyms** Write the list word that means the same as the words in each group below.

15. state, predicament, ___
16. job, career, ___
17. resolve, purpose, ___
18. mother, grandmother, ___
19. goal, target, ___
20. interest, concentration, ___

1. _____
2. _____
3. _____
4. _____
5. _____
6. _____
7. _____
8. _____
9. _____
10. _____
11. _____
12. _____
13. _____
14. _____
15. _____
16. _____
17. _____
18. _____
19. _____
20. _____

Everyday Spelling © Scott Foresman • Addison Wesley

Challenge Words

succotash   artichoke   sauerkraut   won ton   chutney

■ Use Challenge Words and the list of clues to complete the puzzle below. Then read the word in the dark box that tells about all these foods.

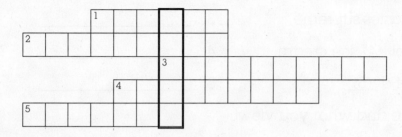

Foods of the World
1. Chinese
2. Native American
3. German
4. Italian
5. Indian

■ New foods can add zest to the dinner table and spice to life. Use one or more Challenge Words to describe a special feast, a new food, or food festival you have enjoyed.

_____

_____

_____

_____

_____

_____

_____

_____

23 ■ THINK AND PRACTICE

moose	cobra	alligator	vanilla	banana
tomato	mustard	hula	picnic	barbecue

■ **Complete a Poem** Write list words to complete the poem.

Yellow _(1)_ on a hot dog bun,

An old _(2)_ table in the sun.

A ripe red _(3)_ tastes supreme,

Followed by cool _(4)_ ice cream.

Part of the fun of a _(5)_

Is what you taste and what you view!

1. _____

2. _____

3. _____

4. _____

5. _____

■ **Classifying** Write the list word that belongs in each group.

6. waltz, jig, _____

7. apple, pear, _____

8. crocodile, lizard, _____

9. copperhead, rattlesnake, _____

10. reindeer, elk, _____

11. chocolate, strawberry, _____

STRATEGIC SPELLING: Using the Divide and Conquer Strategy

Write four list words that are hard for you. Draw lines between
the syllables. Check the Spelling Dictionary if you need help.
Then study the words syllable by syllable.

12. _____   14. _____

13. _____   15. _____

Everyday Spelling © Scott Foresman • Addison Wesley

Name _____

Word List

moose	cobra	alligator	vanilla	banana
tomato	mustard	hula	picnic	barbecue
crocodile	coyote	koala	macaroni	catsup
polka	ballet	waltz	banquet	buffet

■ **Analogies** Use a list word to complete each analogy below.

1. Bark is to dog as howl is to ___.
2. Green is to relish as red is to ___.
3. Oven is to bake as grill is to ___.
4. Suffocate is to boa constrictor as poison is to ___.
5. Informal is to picnic as formal is to ___.
6. Rind is to orange as skin is to ___.
7. Folk dance is to square dance as ballroom dance is to ___.
8. United States is to eagle as Australia is to ___.
9. Dairy product is to milk as flavoring is to ___.
10. Mexico is to hat dance as Hawaii is to ___.

■ **Making Inferences** Write a list word to match each clue below.

11. You need to stand on tiptoe to do this.
12. This is a seedy sort of food.
13. You'll share this with ants.
14. This will spice up your meal.
15. Have all you can eat, but serve yourself.
16. This creature has a lot of headgear.
17. If you can hop to it, you'll do fine.
18. This goes best with cheese.
19. See you later, ___.
20. In a while, ___.

1. _____
2. _____
3. _____
4. _____
5. _____
6. _____
7. _____
8. _____
9. _____
10. _____
11. _____
12. _____
13. _____
14. _____
15. _____
16. _____
17. _____
18. _____
19. _____
20. _____

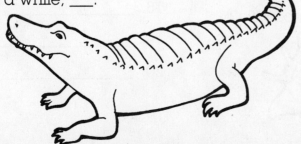

Everyday Spelling © Scott Foresman • Addison Wesley

23 ■ REVIEW

Word List

moose	cobra	alligator	vanilla	banana
tomato	mustard	hula	picnic	barbecue
crocodile	coyote	koala	macaroni	catsup
polka	ballet	waltz	banquet	buffet

■ **Analogies** Write the list word that completes each analogy.

1. Crisp is to apple as juicy is to ___.
2. Chicken is to fry as steak is to ___.
3. Platter is to dinner as basket is to ___.
4. Cobbler is to peach as cream pie is to ___.
5. Bear is to grizzly as snake is to ___.
6. Food is to flavoring as yogurt is to ___.
7. Guitar is to jitterbug as accordion is to ___.
8. Horn is to buffalo as antler is to ___.
9. Corsage is to prom as lei is to ___.
10. Apple is to applesauce as tomato is to ___.

■ **Definitions** Write the list word that answers each question.

11. What word is a big meal that is served?
12. What word is a prairie wolf?
13. What word is a yellow sauce?
14. What word is an old-fashioned, slow dance?
15. What reptile looks like an alligator?
16. What word is a furry Australian?
17. What word toe-dances?
18. What word often comes with a long, strong table?
19. What word is tubes of pasta?
20. What reptile is similar to a crocodile?

1. _____
2. _____
3. _____
4. _____
5. _____
6. _____
7. _____
8. _____
9. _____
10. _____
11. _____
12. _____
13. _____
14. _____
15. _____
16. _____
17. _____
18. _____
19. _____
20. _____

Everyday Spelling © Scott Foresman • Addison Wesley

Name _____

Lesson 19				
different	variety	favorite	sentence	instance

■ **Alpha Order** Write the list word that fits alphabetically in each group.

1. senior _____ separate

2. fault _____ fawn

3. diesel _____ difficult

4. inspect _____ instrument

5. vapor _____ vary

Lesson 20				
tunnel	propeller	collector	single	slogan

■ **Riddles** Write the list word that answers each riddle.

1. I end with **er** and am found on a helicopter. _____

2. I end with **an** and am a saying. _____

3. I end with **le** and mean "one." _____

4. I end with **el** and go through a mountain. _____

5. I end with **or** and like to save things. _____

Lesson 21				
worth	disturb	expert	report	ignore

■ **Classifying** Write the list word that has the same spelling and vowel sound as the words in each group.

1. service, nerve, _____

2. thorn, foreign, _____

3. nurse, turn, _____

4. explore, deplore, _____

5. attorney, thorough, _____

Everyday Spelling © Scott Foresman • Addison Wesley

Name _____

24B ■ REVIEW

Lesson 22

| exploration | occupation | convention | collection | television |

■ **Word Forms** Add **-ation**, **-tion**, or **-ion** to each word to create a list word.

1. televise _____

2. occupy _____

3. explore _____

4. convene _____

5. collect _____

Lesson 23

| alligator | vanilla | tomato | mustard | picnic |

■ **Drawing Conclusions** Write the list word that matches each clue.

1. Combine me with lettuce to make a salad. _____

2. Squirt me on a hot dog. _____

3. Choose me as an ice cream flavor. _____

4. Enjoy me as an outdoor feast. _____

5. Watch out for my jaws full of sharp teeth. _____

Name _____

Challenge Words
antidote   counterfeit   environmental   guarantee   sophomore

■ Write a Challenge Word for each clue.

1. _____: counteracts a poison

2. _____: has one year fewer than a junior

3. _____: shows thought for the earth

4. _____: can take the risk out of buying a product

5. _____: phony; not real

■ The rain forests of the world are important to our environment. Use one or more Challenge Words to write a description of a rain forest, or an account of an expedition into a rain forest.

_____

_____

_____

_____

_____

_____

_____

_____

Everyday Spelling © Scott Foresman • Addison Wesley

25 ■ THINK AND PRACTICE

| probably | cabinet | separate | wondering | clothes |
| temperature | average | beginning | restaurant | promise |

■ **Associations** Write the list word that is associated with each item.

1. maybe _____

2. chef _____

3. ending _____

4. weather _____

5. fashions _____

■ **Context Clues** Complete each sentence with a list word.

6. Linda made a _____ that she would write to me.

7. The girls were _____ whether it would rain.

8. At the _____ of each day, Mr. Santiago makes announcements to the students.

9. The Browns' _____ grocery bill is $125 per week.

10. Each sister has a _____ bedroom.

11. The plates are in the kitchen _____ by the door.

STRATEGIC SPELLING: Pronouncing for Spelling

We sometimes spell words wrong because we say them wrong. Write *probably*, *cabinet*, *temperature*, and *wondering*. Now say each word slowly and carefully. Be sure to pronounce the sounds of the underlined letters.

12. _____   14. _____

13. _____   15. _____

Everyday Spelling © Scott Foresman • Addison Wesley

Word List

probably	cabinet	separate	wondering	clothes
temperature	average	beginning	restaurant	promise
aspirin	desperate	awfully	fishhook	twelfth
skiing	unwritten	roughly	schedule	overrule

■ **Classifying** Write the list word that belongs in each group below.

1. rod, reel, ___
2. pills, medicine, ___
3. cupboard, closet, ___
4. tenth, eleventh, ___
5. pledge, vow, ___
6. heat, measurement, ___
7. harshly, severely, ___
8. sledding, tobogganing, ___
9. outfits, garments, ___
10. diner, cafeteria, ___
11. timetable, directory, ___
12. divide, split up, ___

■ **Word Hints** Use the underlined word in each sentence to help you find the correct list word. Write each word.

13. This character would ___ never rob anyone.
14. We beg you, start at the ___.
15. I'm ___ sorry I can't eat more, but I'm too full.
16. He was so ___ he ate all the sandwiches.
17. We think you did err to ___ the vote.
18. Rae can't turn in her theme because it is ___.
19. Heather was in a rage over her ___ grade.
20. I was ___ if you would ring me today.

1. _____
2. _____
3. _____
4. _____
5. _____
6. _____
7. _____
8. _____
9. _____
10. _____
11. _____
12. _____
13. _____
14. _____
15. _____
16. _____
17. _____
18. _____
19. _____
20. _____

Name _____

Word List

probably	cabinet	separate	wondering	clothes
temperature	average	beginning	restaurant	promise
aspirin	desperate	awfully	fishhook	twelfth
skiing	unwritten	roughly	schedule	overrule

■ **Synonyms** Write the list word that means the same as each word or phrase below.

1. terribly
2. likely
3. apart
4. so-so
5. starting
6. pledge
7. diner
8. wardrobe
9. cupboard
10. puzzling over
11. forlorn

■ **Word Search** Find the nine list words in the puzzle. They may be printed across or down. Write them.

```
t  e  m  p  e  r  a  t  u  r  e
u  n  w  r  i  t  t  e  n  l  n
t  w  e  l  f  t  h  s  m  y  g
w  t  d  a  f  u  t  c  t  s  r
o  b  v  s  e  s  n  h  u  o  i
v  e  s  p  c  l  k  e  b  p  q
e  s  k  i  i  n  g  d  h  l  n
r  a  h  r  k  m  c  u  q  o  m
r  j  g  i  o  v  b  l  z  p  l
u  k  i  n  r  p  h  e  u  o  n
l  f  i  s  h  h  o  o  k  r  o
e  l  a  d  t  i  t  o  d  e  a
b  r  r  o  u  g  h  l  y  m  l
```

1. _____
2. _____
3. _____
4. _____
5. _____
6. _____
7. _____
8. _____
9. _____
10. _____
11. _____
12. _____
13. _____
14. _____
15. _____
16. _____
17. _____
18. _____
19. _____
20. _____

Everyday Spelling © Scott Foresman • Addison Wesley

Challenge Words

comparative   apprenticeship   compassionate   alienate   appreciative

■ Use Challenge Words from the list above to complete the following sentences.

1. We did a _____ study of prices before we bought this bike.

2. I feel deeply _____ for all of your help.

3. Don't _____ the dog by teasing him.

4. Her _____ helped her learn a lot about mixing paint.

5. The doctor's _____ care helped the patient feel better.

■ Learning a new craft or skill can be a great adventure. Write a paragraph about a girl or boy who gets a chance to learn from a master. Use one or more Challenge Words in your narrative.

_____

_____

_____

_____

_____

_____

_____

_____

_____

_____

26 ■ THINK AND PRACTICE

originate	fortunate	activate	attractive	inventive
negative	creative	friendship	championship	leadership

■ **Antonyms** Write the list word that means the opposite
of each word.

1. positive   _____

2. unlucky   _____

3. unappealing   _____

4. finish   _____

■ **Adding Suffixes** Add a suffix to each word in parentheses
to form a list word that completes the sentence.

5. (champion)   The soccer team won the city _____.

6. (leader)   President Roosevelt was known for his _____
during World War II.

7. (invent)   A very _____ student won first prize
at the science fair.

8. (create)   Van Gogh was a _____ painter.

9. (active)   Do you know how to _____ the house's
alarm system?

10. (friend)   The _____ between the gorilla and
the kitten amazed everyone who saw it.

11. (origin)   The bicycle race will _____ in Sioux City,
Iowa, and finish in Chicago, Illinois.

STRATEGIC SPELLING: Building New Words
To make new words, add one of the suffixes to each
of these base words: *partner, select, citizen, effect.*

Add -ship   **Add -ive**

12. _____   14. _____

13. _____   15. _____

Everyday Spelling © Scott Foresman • Addison Wesley

Name _____

Word List

originate	fortunate	activate	attractive
inventive	negative	creative	friendship
championship	leadership	affectionate	considerate
obligate	productive	defective	constructive
ownership	membership	hardship	relationship

■ **Making Inferences** Write a list word to match each clue below.

1. a new bike whose brakes don't work
2. feeling lucky
3. chronic illness
4. being part of a club
5. a clothing model
6. winning the playoff game
7. giving commands
8. cuddling a cat or dog
9. being an owner
10. shaking one's head "no"

1. _____

2. _____

3. _____

4. _____

5. _____

6. _____

7. _____

8. _____

9. _____

10. _____

■ **Puzzle** Fill in the blanks with list words. The letters in the circles will answer the riddle.

11. __ __ __ (__) **d** __ __ __ __

12. __ **r** __ __ (__) __ __ __

13. __ **c** __ __ (__) __ __ __

14. __ __ __ (__) __ **d** __ __

15. __ __ **l** __ __ __ (__) __ __

16. **p** __ __ __ __ (__) __ __

17. __ __ __ **s** __ __ __ (__) __ __

18. __ __ __ **t** __ (__) __

19. __ **b** __ __ __ __ (__)

What do you have to be in order to solve puzzles?

20. __ __ __ __ __ __ __ __ __ __

26 ■ REVIEW

Word List

originate	fortunate	activate	attractive
inventive	negative	creative	friendship
championship	leadership	affectionate	considerate
obligate	productive	defective	constructive
ownership	membership	hardship	relationship

■ **The Riddle Ship** Write the list word that answers each riddle.

1. What *ship* is for presidents?
2. What *ship* is for clubs and groups?
3. What *ship* is for Super Bowl winners?
4. What *ship* is for rocks?
5. What *ship* is for family?
6. What *ship* has a possessive atmosphere?
7. What *ship* likes all the other ships?

■ **Synonyms** Write the list word that means the same as the underlined word or phrase.

8. The new toaster is <u>broken</u>.
9. Remembering to call was <u>thoughtful</u> of you.
10. That hairdo is <u>good-looking</u> on you.
11. You <u>turn on</u> the machine by pushing that button.
12. Will the contract <u>force</u> us to make future purchases?
13–14. Make at least some of the criticism <u>positive</u> rather than <u>unfavorable</u>.

■ **Adding Endings** Write the list words formed by adding **-ive** or **-ate.**

15. product + ive
16. origin + ate
17. create + ive
18. fortune + ate
19. invent + ive
20. affection + ate

1. _____
2. _____
3. _____
4. _____
5. _____
6. _____
7. _____
8. _____
9. _____
10. _____
11. _____
12. _____
13. _____
14. _____
15. _____
16. _____
17. _____
18. _____
19. _____
20. _____

Everyday Spelling © Scott Foresman • Addison Wesley

```
                        Challenge Words
  internally   posthumous   premonition   underachiever   overemphasize
```

■ Write a Challenge Word for each definition.

1. inside _____

2. give too much emphasis _____

3. happening after death _____

4. works below level of ability _____

5. a forewarning _____

■ Some people are quiet and shy about their accomplishments. Write a paragraph about a quiet person who has secretly done amazing things. Use one or more Challenge Words in your paragraph.

_____

_____

_____

_____

_____

_____

_____

_____

_____

_____

_____

_____

27 ■ THINK AND PRACTICE

pretrial	prearrange	postdate	postwar	overcook
overlook	overflow	undercover	include	exclude

■ **Definitions** Write the list word that fits each definition.

1. to make preparations ahead of time _____

2. after a period of armed conflict _____

3. to heat a food for too long _____

4. in the time before a legal case goes to court _____

5. to bar from participation _____

■ **Context Clues** Complete each sentence with a list word.

6. Be sure to _____ a title page with your report.

7. The novel is about a British _____ agent in World War I.

8. The pond will _____ if it rains any more.

9. The Laus' new house will _____ the canyon.

10. It is wise to _____ a ride home from the party.

11. To _____ the check, Amy wrote tomorrow's date on it.

STRATEGIC SPELLING: Building New Words

Make new words by adding one of the prefixes to each
of these base words: *ground, load, crowded, water*.

Add over-   **Add under-**

12. _____   14. _____

13. _____   15. _____

Everyday Spelling © Scott Foresman • Addison Wesley

Name _____

Word List

pretrial	prearrange	postdate	postwar
overcook	overlook	overflow	undercover
include	exclude	premeditated	prehistoric
precaution	postponement	postgraduate	overpopulated
undernourished	underweight	inhale	exhale

■ **Hints** Write the list word that each phrase makes you think of.

1. too many people in a small space
2. wearing a disguise
3. puff out air
4. working together after fighting
5. burn a meal
6. set up a schedule
7. smell a rose
8. going past college graduation
9. lawyers meeting before a hearing
10. too few fruits and vegetables
11. a tool from stone age times

■ **Puzzle** Write list words in the blanks to match the definitions. The letters in the circle will spell the answer to the question.

1. _____
2. _____
3. _____
4. _____
5. _____
6. _____
7. _____
8. _____
9. _____
10. _____
11. _____

12. write a later date __ __ __ **t** __ __ (__) __
13. too thin __ __ __ __ __ **w** __ (__) __
14. fail to see __ __(__)__ __ __ __ **k**
15. a putting off (__)__ **s** __ __ __ __ __ __ __ __
16. foresight __(__)__ **c** __ __ __ __ __
17. contain __ **n** __ __ __ (__)__
18. flood __ __ __ __(__)__ __ **w**
19. planned ahead __ __ __ **m** __(__)__ __ __ __ __
20. leave out __(__)__ **l** __ __ __

Which part of an unfamiliar word might help you figure out its meaning?

__ __ __ __   __ __ __ __ __ __

Everyday Spelling © Scott Foresman • Addison Wesley

27 ■ REVIEW

Word List

pretrial	prearrange	postdate	postwar
overcook	overlook	overflow	undercover
include	exclude	premeditated	prehistoric
precaution	postponement	postgraduate	overpopulated
undernourished	underweight	inhale	exhale

■ **Word Meanings** Write the list word that completes each phrase.

1. ___ the fragrance
2. ___ agent
3. ___ animal
4. ___ studies
5. ___ action

■ **Word Math** Complete each equation to make a list word.

6. over + bake = ___
7. pre + warning = ___
8. over + stream = ___
9. pre + set = ___
10. under + fed = ___
11. post + military conflict = ___
12. over + peopled = ___
13. pre + ordeal = ___
14. under + heaviness = ___
15. post + appointment = ___
16. over + glance = ___

■ **Context Clues** Write the list word that completes each sentence. Say each word carefully to help you spell it.

17. When you want to relax, ___ slowly.
18. Try to ___ a student from each homeroom.
19. The ballgame's ___ means a double-header tomorrow.
20. Budgeting families are trying to ___ as much as possible from shopping lists.

1. _____
2. _____
3. _____
4. _____
5. _____
6. _____
7. _____
8. _____
9. _____
10. _____
11. _____
12. _____
13. _____
14. _____
15. _____
16. _____
17. _____
18. _____
19. _____
20. _____

Everyday Spelling © Scott Foresman • Addison Wesley

Challenge Words

intercept	interception	individual
individuality	cooperate	cooperation

■ Complete the following sentences using the correct forms of the Challenge Words.

1. Each person is an _____. Our clothes, our faces, and

   even the way we walk show our _____.

2. Since you volunteered to take part in this clean-up, I expect

   _____. I hope you all intend to _____ fully.

3. Coach, that was an _____ ! I saw her

   _____ the ball!

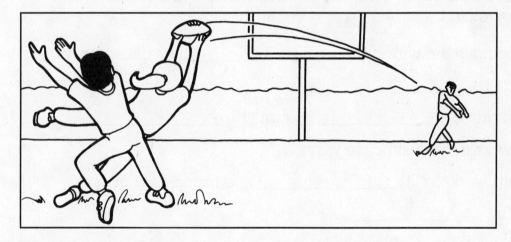

■ In most cases, working together helps to get a project done. Write a paragraph describing the way people work together to accomplish a goal. Use one or more Challenge Words.

_____

_____

_____

_____

_____

Everyday Spelling © Scott Foresman • Addison Wesley

Name _____

28 ■ THINK AND PRACTICE

direct	direction	history	historical	fact
factual	critic	criticize	produce	production

■ **Word Relationships** Write the list word that matches each clue. Then write the list word that is related to it.

the study of past events

1. _____ 2. _____

something that can be proven true or false

3. _____ 4. _____

one who evaluates a movie, play, or other work of art

5. _____ 6. _____

■ **Related Pairs** To complete each sentence, write two list words that are related.

After going in the wrong (7) _____, we asked Amy

to (8) _____ us.

A good art (9) _____ can (10) _____

a work in a constructive way.

It is hard work to (11) _____ a brand-new musical

(12) _____.

STRATEGIC SPELLING: Seeing Meaning Connections

Complete the paragraph with words from the box.

Words related to produce		
product	producer	unproductive

The motion-picture (13) _____ was upset. He had

watched the movie crew spend an (14) _____ day

trying to shoot an important scene. No one was pleased with the

finished (15) _____. The entire scene would have to

be reshot tomorrow.

Everyday Spelling © Scott Foresman • Addison Wesley

108

Name _____

Word List

direct	direction	history	historical	fact
factual	critic	criticize	produce	production
magic	magician	electric	electrician	distract
distraction	remedy	remedial	origin	original

■ **Making New Words** Write the list word that is formed when you combine the synonym for each word or phrase below with the ending.

1. charged with energy + ian = _____

2. guide + ion = _____

3. source + al = _____

4. disturb + ion = _____

5. cure + ial = _____

6. make + tion = _____

7. past events + ical = _____

8. hocus pocus + ian = _____

9. statistic + ual = _____

10. reviewer + ize = _____

ELECTRICAL WORK

■ **Base Words** Write the list word that is the base word for each word below.

11. origins _____

12. misdirected _____

13. distracted _____

14. magically _____

15. factor _____

16. producing _____

17. electrical _____

18. historian _____

19. remedied _____

20. critical _____

Name _____

28 ■ REVIEW

Word List

direct	direction	history	historical	fact
factual	critic	criticize	produce	production
magic	magician	electric	electrician	distract
distraction	remedy	remedial	origin	original

■ **Definition Pairs** Write the list words that fit each set of definitions.

1–2. reality/true
3–4. cure/healing
5–6. make/manufacturing
7–8. source/innovative
9–10. divert/interruption
11–12. straight/orientation

■ **Multiple Meanings** Write the list word that completes each phrase.

13. ancient ___
14. ___ marker
15. my own worst ___
16. ___ era
17. ___ light bulb

■ **Drawing Conclusions** Write the list word that answers each question.

18. Who pulls rabbits out of hats?
19. What do reviewers do both positively and negatively?
20. Who keeps currents flowing?

1. _____

2. _____

3. _____

4. _____

5. _____

6. _____

7. _____

8. _____

9. _____

10. _____

11. _____

12. _____

13. _____

14. _____

15. _____

16. _____

17. _____

18. _____

19. _____

20. _____

Everyday Spelling © Scott Foresman • Addison Wesley

Challenge Words
sometimes   some times   backwards   pocketful   underneath

■ Use Challenge Words to complete the puzzle.

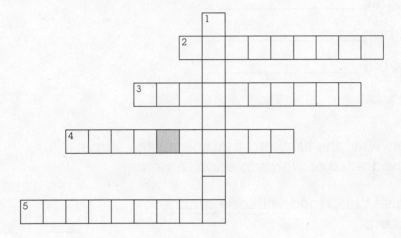

Across
2. a filled pouch
3. below
4. certain occasions
5. wrong way around

Down
1. now and then

■ Think about a pocketful of treasures. It could be a collection. It could be a group of lucky charms. Write a description of the treasures using one or more Challenge Words.

_____

_____

_____

_____

_____

_____

29 ■ THINK AND PRACTICE

a lot	want to	all ways	always	away
a way	a little	below	because	together

■ **Antonyms** Write the list word that completes each phrase.

1. not above, but _____

2. not never, but _____

3. not apart, but _____

4. not a little, but _____

5. not toward, but _____

■ **Definitions** Write the list word that means the same as the underlined word or words in each sentence.

6. Two violinists performed <u>with one another</u> at the concert.   _____

7. The gymnasts <u>desire to</u> compete at the Olympics.   _____

8. The recipe calls for <u>a tiny bit of</u> hot pepper sauce.   _____

9. The club will find <u>a means</u> to raise money for the trip.   _____

10. <u>Since</u> she was late, she missed the best part of the play.   _____

11. Rosa tried <u>every method</u> of training her dog.   _____

12. Look <u>in another direction</u> when the movie is scary.   _____

STRATEGIC SPELLING: Seeing Meaning Connections

Write the word that fits each definition.

Words with *way*		
away	always	wayward

13. at all times _____

14. resisting authority or control _____

15. from this or that place _____

Everyday Spelling © Scott Foresman • Addison Wesley

Word List

a lot	want to	all ways	always	away
a way	a little	below	because	together
forget	around	a while	awhile	forever
again	tonight	tomorrow	become	going to

■ Riddles Use pairs or groups of confusing words to match the clues below.

1. a teaspoon of sand
2. a beach full of sand
3. the next morning
4. this very evening
5. in cooperation, either time
6. this way, that way, and the other way
7. now, next week, and all the time
8. a circular movement
9. you *gain* when you do something over and over
10. out of sight and at a distance
11. a method
12. a word to tell you about something *lower*
13. a word that means *for this reason*
14. a word that means *come to be*, but turns it around
15. how some people *wish* for action
16. how other people *make a plan* for action
17. the opposite of *remember*
18. a synonym for *always*
19. a time—the object of a preposition
20. also a time—an adverb

1. _____
2. _____
3. _____
4. _____
5. _____
6. _____
7. _____
8. _____
9. _____
10. _____
11. _____
12. _____
13. _____
14. _____
15. _____
16. _____
17. _____
18. _____
19. _____
20. _____

29 ■ REVIEW

Word List

a lot	want to	all ways	always	away
a way	a little	below	because	together
forget	around	a while	awhile	forever
again	tonight	tomorrow	become	going to

■ **Classifying** Write the list word that belongs in each group.

1. yesterday, today, ___
2. desire to, wish to, ___
3. a bit, a smidgen, ___
4. heading for, aiming toward, ___
5. about, approximately, ___
6. a ton, a heap, ___
7. missing, absent, ___
8. develop, evolve, ___
9. over, once more, ___
10. since, whereas, ___
11. every means, total methods, ___
12. a means, a method, ___

■ **Antonyms** Write the list word that means the opposite of each underlined word.

13. The girls decided to go to the dance separately.
14. The recital is taking place today.
15. Sheila did remember to water the lawn.

■ **Multiple Meanings** Write the list word that completes each phrase or sentence.

16. ___ yours
17. Look out ___!
18. Stop in for ___.
19. as ___
20. dream ___ with me

1. _____
2. _____
3. _____
4. _____
5. _____
6. _____
7. _____
8. _____
9. _____
10. _____
11. _____
12. _____
13. _____
14. _____
15. _____
16. _____
17. _____
18. _____
19. _____
20. _____

Everyday Spelling © Scott Foresman • Addison Wesley

Lesson 25

probably   separate   cabinet   beginning   restaurant

■ **Making Inferences** Write the list word that completes each phrase.

1. not the end or the middle but the _____

2. not a closet or a cupboard but a _____

3. not definitely or certainly but _____

4. not a cafe or a diner but a _____

5. not joined or together but _____

Lesson 26

friendship   championship   attractive   inventive   originate

■ **Word Forms** Write the list word that has each meaning and ending indicated below.

1. winner + ship   _____

2. beginning + ate   _____

3. draw to + ive   _____

4. someone you like + ship _____

5. to think up + ive   _____

Lesson 27

overcook   pretrial   postdate   include   exclude

■ **Antonyms** Write the list word that means the opposite of each word.

1. predate   _____

2. exclude   _____

3. undercook   _____

4. include   _____

5. posttrial   _____

30B ■ REVIEW

Lesson 28

factual	direction	criticize	historical	production

■ **Context** Write the list word that is related to the underlined word and completes each sentence.

1. It is the job of a <u>critic</u> to _____.

2. I like <u>history</u>, so I read _____ novels.

3. If you rely on <u>fact</u>, not opinion, you are being _____.

4. <u>Direct</u> the hikers by pointing in the right _____.

5. Our group plans to <u>produce</u> a musical _____ next fall.

Lesson 29

always	all ways	away	a lot	together

■ **Definitions** Write the list word that fits the definition.

1. at a distance _____

2. all directions _____

3. a great many _____

4. with each other _____

5. at all times _____

Everyday Spelling © Scott Foresman • Addison Wesley

> **Challenge Words**
>
> temperamental   parliament   cantaloupe   archaeology   nuisance

■ Write a Challenge Word to match each clue below.

1. a tendency to get angry _____

2. a kind of melon _____

3. a meeting of lawmakers _____

4. a science about the past _____

5. a bother _____

■ Did you ever want to be an archaeologist? Use one or more Challenge Words to write a paragraph comparing and contrasting jobs you might like.

_____

_____

_____

_____

_____

_____

_____

_____

Name _____

31 ■ THINK AND PRACTICE

interested	usually	American	toward	business
vegetable	really	opposite	difficult	Christmas

■ **Synonyms** Write the list word that means the same as each word.

1. truly _____

2. hard _____

3. intrigued _____

4. antonym _____

5. trade _____

6. near _____

■ **Analogies** Write the list word that completes each analogy.

7. Peach is to fruit as carrot is to _____.

8. November is to Thanksgiving as December is to _____.

9. Amusement park is to pleasure as office is to _____.

10. Seldom is to infrequently as commonly is to _____.

11. Italy is to Italian as United States is to _____.

12. Happy is to sad as bored is to _____.

13. Easy is to simple as troublesome is to _____.

STRATEGIC SPELLING: Choosing the Best Strategy

Write two list words that you find hard to spell. Which strategy could help you spell each word? Name the strategy and tell why you chose it. Then compare choices with a partner. For a list of strategies, see page 142.

14. _____ _____

_____

15. _____ _____

_____

Everyday Spelling © Scott Foresman • Addison Wesley

Word List

interested	usually	American	toward	business
vegetable	really	opposite	difficult	Christmas
magazine	apologize	multiply	jealousy	elementary
oxygen	Maryland	sensitive	laughter	disease

■ **Analogies** Write a list word to complete each analogy below.

1. Kiwi is to fruit as eggplant is to ___.
2. Weary is to energetic as bored is to ___.
3. Mexico is to Mexican as America is to ___.
4. *Daily Planet* is to newspaper as *Newsweek* is to ___.
5. Solid is to ice as gas is to ___.
6. Effortless is to simple as laborious is to ___.
7. City is to Baltimore as state is to ___.
8. Add is to subtract as divide is to ___.
9. Jewish is to Hannukah as Christian is to ___.
10. Sadness is to weeping as happiness is to ___.

■ **Hidden Words** Write the list word that matches each description below. Use the underlined word as a clue.

11. You probably feel <u>lousy</u> when you have this emotion.
12. People should not have to do this when they play <u>polo</u>.
13. Do you take a <u>bus</u> to this place?
14. A tugboat has to <u>tow</u> a boat this way to reach shore.
15. Reading is an <u>element</u> of this kind of school.
16. You're not at <u>ease</u> when you have this.

These two words must be friends because they both contain the word <u>ally</u>.

17. _____   18. _____

These two words probably <u>sit</u> around talking about their meanings.

19. _____   20. _____

1. _____
2. _____
3. _____
4. _____
5. _____
6. _____
7. _____
8. _____
9. _____
10. _____
11. _____
12. _____
13. _____
14. _____
15. _____
16. _____

Name _____

31 ■ REVIEW

Word List

interested	usually	American	toward	business
vegetable	really	opposite	difficult	Christmas
magazine	apologize	multiply	jealousy	elementary
oxygen	Maryland	sensitive	laughter	disease

■ **Definitions** Write the list word that is
missing from each person's statement.

1. Scuba diver: "Where are the ___ tanks?"
2. Soldier: "I can fold the ___ flag correctly."
3. Salesperson: "Are you ___ in a wool coat?"
4. Model: "I model in a weekly fashion ___."
5. Doctor: "Finding a cure for that disease is going
   to be extremely ___."
6. Cadet: "The naval academy is in Annapolis,
   ___."
7. Teacher: "I've taught all the ___ grades."
8. Mathematician: "Whenever you ___ by zero,
   you get zero."
9. Poet: "People like my ___ verses about human
   emotions."
10. Optimist: "I ___, though not always, have high
    hopes."

■ **Syllables** Each column of letters is one
syllable of a two-syllable word. Match the
syllables and write the list words.

11. laugh	ness
12. dis	ter
13. to	mas
14. Christ	ease
15. busi	ward

■ **Hidden Words** Each word below is hidden
in a list word. Write the list word.

16. lousy	19. site
17. polo	20. real
18. table	

1. _____
2. _____
3. _____
4. _____
5. _____
6. _____
7. _____
8. _____
9. _____
10. _____
11. _____
12. _____
13. _____
14. _____
15. _____
16. _____
17. _____
18. _____
19. _____
20. _____

Everyday Spelling © Scott Foresman • Addison Wesley

Name _____

Challenge Words

irrelevant   illiterate   immeasurable   inconsiderate   inequality

---

■ Write the Challenge Word that goes with each clue below.

1. not able to read   _____

2. not to the point   _____

3. not concerned with fairness   _____

4. not thoughtful   _____

5. not countable   _____

■ Imagine that your class has the opportunity to win a trip to the nation's capital. Use Challenge Words to write a paragraph that tells why your class should be chosen for the trip.

_____

_____

_____

_____

_____

_____

_____

_____

_____

_____

_____

_____

_____

Everyday Spelling © Scott Foresman • Addison Wesley

Name _____

32 ■ THINK AND PRACTICE

illegal	inexpensive	inaccurate	indirect	informal
impolite	improper	imperfect	irresponsible	irregular

■ **Context** Write the list word that is missing from each person's statement.

1. Hostess: "Dress casually for my _____ party."

2. Salesperson: "This is an _____ way to update your wardrobe."

3. Parent: "It is _____ to forget to write a thank-you note."

4. Police Officer: "It is _____ to exceed the speed limit."

5. Mathematician: "The answer to this equation is _____."

■ **Synonyms** Write a list word that means about the same as the underlined word or words in each sentence.

6. Drivers will lose their licenses if they are
   not trustworthy.   _____

7. His answer to the teacher's question was
   not straightforward.   _____

8. The shoes were on sale because they were
   not made perfectly.   _____

9. On the map, the coastline looks very uneven.   _____

10. The comedian's joke about his children was
    in poor taste.   _____

11. Amy found a cheap quilt at a garage sale.   _____

STRATEGIC SPELLING: Building New Words
Make new words by adding one of the prefixes to each
of these words: *active, practical, possible, complete.*
Use your Spelling Dictionary if you need help.

Add in-	**Add im-**
12. _____	14. _____
13. _____	15. _____

Everyday Spelling © Scott Foresman • Addison Wesley

Word List

illegal	inexpensive	inaccurate	indirect	informal
impolite	improper	imperfect	irresponsible	irregular
illogical	illegible	incapable	incredible	impatient
imbalance	immature	irrational	irresistible	irreplaceable

■ **Word Building** All the prefixes in this lesson mean *not.* Write the list word that means the same as each prefix and base word definition below.

1. not + able to do something
2. not + sane
3. not + high-priced
4. not + permitted by law
5. not + suitable
6. not + believable
7. not + grown up
8. not + making sense
9. not + correct
10. not + courteous
11. not + able to be read
12. not + one hundred percent

■ **Making Inferences** Write the list word that each phrase makes you think of.

13. feeling dizzy
14. a lost family heirloom
15. leaving your bike in the way
16. a path that goes a roundabout way
17. pants with different leg lengths
18. wearing casual clothing
19. a cool lake on a hot day
20. wanting to get started immediately

1. _____
2. _____
3. _____
4. _____
5. _____
6. _____
7. _____
8. _____
9. _____
10. _____
11. _____
12. _____
13. _____
14. _____
15. _____
16. _____
17. _____
18. _____
19. _____
20. _____

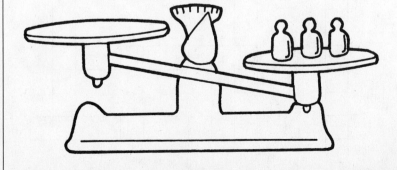

32 ■ REVIEW

Word List

illegal	inexpensive	inaccurate	indirect	informal
impolite	improper	imperfect	irresponsible	irregular
illogical	illegible	incapable	incredible	impatient
imbalance	immature	irrational	irresistible	irreplaceable

■ Analogies Write the list words to complete the analogies.

1. Correct is to right as wrong is to ___.
2. Rich is to costly as cheap is to ___.
3. Sun is to credible as flying saucer is to ___.
4. Law is to legal as speeding is to ___.
5. Quiet is to patient as fidget is to ___
6. Tree is to mature as seed is to ___.
7. Reasonable is to logical as unreasonable is to ___.
8. Sane is to rational as crazy is to ___.
9. Top hat is to formal as jeans are to ___.
10. Can is to cannot as capable is to ___.
11. Mannerly is to proper as vulgar is to ___.

■ Building New Words Make new words by adding the prefix **ir-** to these base words. Use your Spelling Dictionary if you need help.

12. responsible
13. replaceable
14. resistible

1. _____
2. _____
3. _____
4. _____
5. _____
6. _____
7. _____
8. _____
9. _____
10. _____
11. _____
12. _____
13. _____
14. _____

■ Puzzle Use the clues to help you fill in the puzzle with list words.

Across
2. inequality
4. random
5. rude

Down
1. unreadable
2. defective
3. roundabout

Challenge Words
significance   incompetence   disinfectant   disobedient   concurrent

■ Use Challenge Words to complete the relationships described below.

1. _____ is to consecutive as rich is to poor.

2. _____ is to law-abiding as hungry is to well-fed.

3. _____ is to excellence as bumbling is to grace.

4. _____ is to germs as medicine is to bacteria.

5. _____ is to importance as sadness is to gloom.

■ Sometimes, taking responsibility brings more than you bargained for. Use one or more Challenge Words to write a paragraph about a baby-sitting, dog-sitting, or house-sitting job that wasn't as easy as it seemed.

_____

_____

_____

_____

_____

_____

_____

_____

_____

_____

_____

_____

_____

33 ■ THINK AND PRACTICE

entrance	performance	appearance	clearance	independence
difference	excellence	brilliant	important	intelligent

■ **Word Forms** Write the list words that contain these base words.

1. excel _____

2. depend _____

3. differ _____

4. enter _____

5. import _____

■ **Definitions** Write the list word that fits each definition.

6. a public presentation _____

7. outward look _____

8. shining very brightly _____

9. a sale to get rid of stock _____

10. having mental capacity _____

11. the act of coming in _____

STRATEGIC SPELLING: Building New Words

Add the suffix **-ence** or **-ance** to each base word
to make a new word. Check the Spelling Dictionary
if you need help.

Base word	New word
12. exist	_____
13. inherit	_____
14. refer	_____
15. attend	_____

Everyday Spelling © Scott Foresman • Addison Wesley

Word List

entrance	performance	appearance	clearance
independence	difference	excellence	brilliant
important	intelligent	insurance	confidence
coincidence	pollutant	ignorant	hesitant
apparent	persistent	convenient	consistent

■ **Pronunciations** Write a list word for each pronunciation.

1. (kən vē′nyənt)
2. (im pôrt′nt)
3. (kon′fə dəns)
4. (bril′yənt)
5. (ə par′ənt)
6. (in tel′ə jənt)
7. (kən sis′tənt)
8. (ig′nər ənt)
9. (kō in′sə dəns)
10. (in′di pen′dəns)

■ **Word Forms** Write the list word that belongs in each group.

11. hesitate, hesitated, ___
12. appear, disappear, ___
13. clearly, unclear, ___
14. persisted, persistence, ___
15. differ, different, ___
16. insured, uninsured, ___
17. entry, entering, ___
18. excelling, excellent, ___
19. unpolluted, polluting, ___
20. perform, performing, ___

1. _____
2. _____
3. _____
4. _____
5. _____
6. _____
7. _____
8. _____
9. _____
10. _____
11. _____
12. _____
13. _____
14. _____
15. _____
16. _____
17. _____
18. _____
19. _____
20. _____

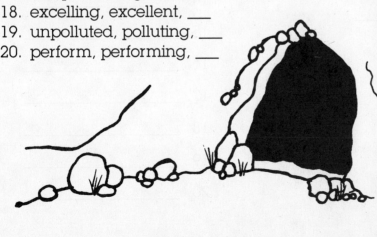

Everyday Spelling © Scott Foresman • Addison Wesley

33 ■ REVIEW

Word List

entrance	performance	appearance	clearance
independence	difference	excellence	brilliant
important	intelligent	insurance	confidence
coincidence	pollutant	ignorant	hesitant
apparent	persistent	convenient	consistent

■ **Word Forms** Combine each base word below with either a suffix or a suffix and prefix to write a list word.

1. clear
2. import
3. persist
4. appear
5. depend
6. excel
7. consist
8. perform
9. confide
10. coincide
11. differ

■ **Antonyms** Write the list word that completes each phrase.

12. not *knowing*, but ___
13. not *camouflaged*, but ___
14. not *exit*, but ___
15. not *certain*, but ___
16. not *out-of-the-way*, but ___
17. not *purifier*, but ___
18. not *dark*, but ___
19. not *stupid*, but ___
20. not *risk*, but ___

1. _____
2. _____
3. _____
4. _____
5. _____
6. _____
7. _____
8. _____
9. _____
10. _____
11. _____
12. _____
13. _____
14. _____
15. _____
16. _____
17. _____
18. _____
19. _____
20. _____

Everyday Spelling © Scott Foresman • Addison Wesley

Challenge Words

vice-president great-grandfather warm-blooded
bookkeeper   headstrong

■ Write the Challenge Words for each clue listed.

1. This one can help you count your money. _____

2. This one can help your country. _____

3. This one can help you learn about your family. _____

4. All mammals are like this. _____

5. All stubborn people are like this. _____

■ America is full of exciting success stories. Use one or more Challenge Words to write a paragraph about an inventor, explorer, artist, or business person you admire. Tell why you think that person is inspiring.

_____

_____

_____

_____

_____

_____

_____

_____

_____

_____

_____

_____

34 ■ THINK AND PRACTICE

basketball	everywhere	outside	summertime	something
baby-sit	roller-skating	drive-in	self-control	part-time

■ **Associations** Write the list word that is associated with each item.

1. self-discipline _____

2. nature _____

3. gymnasium _____

4. August _____

5. rink _____

■ **Drawing Conclusions** Write the list word that answers each question.

6. What is your work schedule if it is not full-time? _____

7. How might you earn money from a family with small children? _____

8. Where could you eat a hamburger in your car? _____

9. Where would you travel if you went all over the world? _____

10. When does the sun shine the longest? _____

11. What would you have if you didn't have nothing? _____

12. What's one way to get around on wheels? _____

STRATEGIC SPELLING: Seeing Meaning Connections
Complete the passage with words from the box.

Words with *drive*		
driver	driveway	drive-in

My older brother is a new (13) _____. On Saturday,

he offered to take me to the (14) _____ burger place

for lunch. I didn't breathe easily until we were back safely in our

own (15) _____!

Everyday Spelling © Scott Foresman • Addison Wesley

Name _____

Word List

basketball	everywhere	outside	summertime
something	baby-sit	roller-skating	drive-in
self-control	part-time	afterthought	cheerleader
quarterback	bookstore	courthouse	ice-skated
ninety-five	brother-in-law	water-skied	old-fashioned

■ **Word Math** Write a list word to match each equation.

1. huddle + signals + football =
2. hoop + dribble + court =
3. ninety + three + two =
4. sister + husband + relative =
5. yells + jumping + uniform =
6. food + window + car =
7. business + reading + buy =
8. infant + care + job =
9. sport + water + towing =
10. lawyers + judge + place =
11. firmness + will power + determination =
12. sport + sidewalk + fast-moving =

■ **Find the Compound** Find two words in each sentence that make up a compound word from the list and write the word.

13. Put these boxes out on the porch on the side away from the weather.
14. She fell on the ice, but then got up and skated away.
15. Every time you lose your hat you ask me where it is!
16. This old rocker was fashioned in 1912.
17. After they went, I thought of something I should have told them.
18. Each summer we make time to visit Grandpa.
19. We'll spend part of Saturday doing chores and the rest of the time hiking.
20. Some days I can't get a thing done.

1. _____
2. _____
3. _____
4. _____
5. _____
6. _____
7. _____
8. _____
9. _____
10. _____
11. _____
12. _____
13. _____
14. _____
15. _____
16. _____
17. _____
18. _____
19. _____
20. _____

Everyday Spelling © Scott Foresman • Addison Wesley

34 ■ REVIEW

Word List

basketball	everywhere	outside	summertime
something	baby-sit	roller-skating	drive-in
self-control	part-time	afterthought	cheerleader
quarterback	bookstore	courthouse	ice-skated
ninety-five	brother-in-law	water-skied	old-fashioned

■ **Hidden Words** Each word below is hidden in a list word. Write the list word.

1. though
2. our
3. ask
4. elf
5. lead
6. thin
7. here
8. net

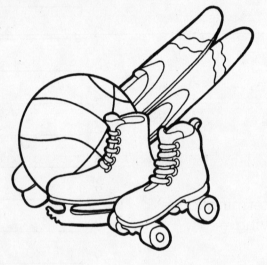

■ **Riddles** Write the list word that answers each riddle.

9. When is all the time a hot time?
10. What's an eight-wheeling sport?
11. What do you do when you sit for, not on?
12. Which fashion is never trendy?
13. Where can you buy shelved ideas?
14. What kind of time is never whole?
15. What's one-fourth of a fullback?

■ **Analogies** Write the list word that completes each phrase.

16. Arena is to wrestled as rink is to ___.
17. Inner is to inside as outer is to ___.
18. Movie is to theater as fast-food is to ___.
19. Helmet is to bicycled as life jacket is to ___.
20. Aunt is to uncle as sister-in-law is to ___.

1. _____
2. _____
3. _____
4. _____
5. _____
6. _____
7. _____
8. _____
9. _____
10. _____
11. _____
12. _____
13. _____
14. _____
15. _____
16. _____
17. _____
18. _____
19. _____
20. _____

Challenge Words

telecommunication   xylophone   autonomy   cacophony   deportation

■ Answer the following questions using Challenge Words.

1. Which word "plugs you in"? _____

2. Which sound is always overwhelming? _____

3. Which word sends you away? _____

4. Which word shows independence? _____

5. Which sound vibrates clearly? _____

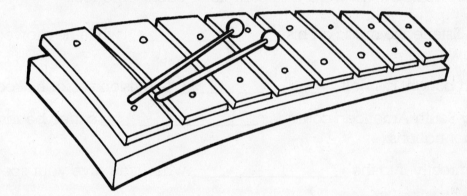

■ Almost everyone has heard a sound that is loud and awful. Use one or more Challenge Words to write a description of your "terrible sound."

_____

_____

_____

_____

_____

_____

_____

_____

Name _____

35 ■ THINK AND PRACTICE

| automobile | autograph | telescope | telecast | telephone |
| microphone | headphones | portable | import | export |

■ **Analogies** Write the list word that completes each analogy.

1. Germs are to microscope as stars are to _____.

2. Fly is to airplane as drive is to _____.

3. Radio is to broadcast as television is to _____.

4. Picture is to photograph as signature is to _____.

5. Write is to typewriter as call is to _____.

■ **Context** Write the list word that completes each sentence.

6. Ryan listened to music on his _____ while he mowed the lawn.

7. Albert bought a small, _____ television set for his room.

8. Many South American countries _____ coffee beans to other nations.

9. Talk directly into the _____ when you give your speech.

10. The United States must _____ much fuel oil from other countries.

STRATEGIC SPELLING: Seeing Meaning Connections

| headlight | headstrong | headline | headband |

11. Write a list word that is related to the words in the box. _____

Write the words from the box that fit the definitions.

12. hard to control or manage _____

13. cloth or ribbon worn around the head _____

14. a bright light at the front of a vehicle _____

15. words in heavy type at the top of an article _____

Name _____

EXTRA PRACTICE ■ 35

Word List

automobile	autograph	telescope	telecast
telephone	microphone	headphones	portable
import	export	automatic	autobiography
autopilot	telegram	telegraph	symphony
saxophone	megaphone	transport	passport

■ **Analogies** Write a list word to complete each analogy below.

1. Taxi is to taxicab as auto is to ___.
2. Car is to license as travel is to ___.
3. Celebrity is to hero as signature is to ___.
4. Other is to biography as self is to ___.
5. String is to violin as reed is to ___.
6. Bugs are to microscope as stars are to ___.
7. Heavy is to stationary as light is to ___.
8. Coach is to team as conductor is to ___.
9. Hotel is to motel as broadcast is to ___.
10. Fridge is to refrigerator as phone is to ___.

■ **Definitions** Use list words to complete each paragraph.

These devices all have to do with sound. An engineer wears (11) during a recording session. A plugged-in (12) allows the human voice to reach a crowd. A (13) can do the same thing but without electricity.

These words all have to do with carrying. An (14) is something carried or sent out of a country. An (15) is brought into a country. The (16) is the method by which the item is carried. This may be a train, a boat, or a plane.

These words have to do with distance. A (17) is a message that comes over a long distance. The (18) is the technological device that carries the message.

These words have to do with things that can move by themselves. A device allows a plane to be guided by itself, without needing a human pilot. It is called an (19). The word is a combination of the words (20) and *pilot*.

1. _____
2. _____
3. _____
4. _____
5. _____
6. _____
7. _____
8. _____
9. _____
10. _____
11. _____
12. _____
13. _____
14. _____
15. _____
16. _____
17. _____
18. _____
19. _____
20. _____

Everyday Spelling © Scott Foresman • Addison Wesley

135

35 ■ REVIEW

Word List

automobile	autograph	telescope	telecast
telephone	microphone	headphones	portable
import	export	automatic	autobiography
autopilot	telegram	telegraph	symphony
saxophone	megaphone	transport	passport

■ **Associations** Write the list word that is associated with each item below.

1. movie star
2. tires
3. voyage to other countries
4. pep rally
5. ear receivers
6. planet
7. music conductor
8. Morse code machine
9. own story
10. truck fleet
11. TV show
12. electronic bank teller
13. ringing device

■ **Definitions** Write the list word that matches each clue.

14. What is a product we buy from another nation?
15. What instrument is named after Adolphe Sax?
16. What's a battery-run TV?
17. What is a wired message?
18. What is a product we sell to another nation?
19. What does an emcee speak into?
20. What helps a jet fly on its own?

1. _____
2. _____
3. _____
4. _____
5. _____
6. _____
7. _____
8. _____
9. _____
10. _____
11. _____
12. _____
13. _____
14. _____
15. _____
16. _____
17. _____
18. _____
19. _____
20. _____

Everyday Spelling © Scott Foresman • Addison Wesley

Name _____

Lesson 31

| interested | toward | usually | difficult | business |

■ **Antonyms** Write the list word that means the opposite of each word or phrase.

1. easy   _____   4. pleasure   _____

2. away from   _____   5. rarely   _____

3. bored   _____

Lesson 32

| illegal | inexpensive | impolite | imperfect | irregular |

■ **Definitions** Write the list word that means the same as the underlined words.

1. A shirt that is <u>not costly</u> is _____.

2. An action <u>not within the law</u> is _____.

3. When something is <u>not exactly right</u>, it is said to be _____.

4. If someone is <u>not mannerly</u>, that person may be _____.

5. A heart with a beat that is <u>not steady</u> has an _____ beat.

Lesson 33

| entrance | appearance | independence | brilliant | intelligent |

■ **Word Forms** Write the list word that has each meaning and suffix indicated below.

Meaning	Suffix	List word
1. freedom from	-ence	_____
2. a place to go in	-ance	_____
3. brightly shining	-ant	_____
4. how one looks	-ance	_____
5. very smart	-ent	_____

Name _____

36B ■ REVIEW

Lesson 34				
outside	everywhere	summertime	drive-in	part-time

■ **Compounds** Find the two words in each sentence that make up a compound word from the list and write the word.

1. I part my hair in the middle some of the time. _____

2. Every pupil wondered where the teacher was. _____

3. Summer is a wonderful time to read. _____

4. We will take a drive in the country. _____

5. Put the dog out in the side yard. _____

Lesson 35				
autograph	telescope	export	portable	headphones

■ **Seeing Relationships** Write the list word or words that match each clue.

1. Has the Greek word part *auto* meaning "self"

1. _____

2. Has the Latin root *phon* meaning "voice" or "sound"

2. _____

3. Has the Greek word part *tele* meaning "far off"

3. _____

4.–5. Have the Latin root *port* meaning "to carry"

4. _____

5. _____

Everyday Spelling © Scott Foresman • Addison Wesley

Answer Key

CHALLENGE ■ 1

Challenge Words				
preliminary	tremendous	mediocre	perception	neutrality

■ Use Challenge Words to complete the puzzle. Fill in the letters going down to spell the word meaning "average."

```
              m
¹t r e m e n d o u s
              d
  ²p r e l i m i n a r y
              o
    ³p e r c e p t i o n
              r
      ⁴n e u t r a l i t y
```

Across
1. huge
2. before starting
3. understanding
4. policy of not being on anyone's side

■ Have you ever seen something that turned out to be different from what you expected? Think about an experience that surprised you in that way. Write a paragraph about it, using one or more Challenge Words.

_____

_____

_____

_____

_____

_____

_____

_____

_____

7

1 ■ THINK AND PRACTICE

poetry	beautiful	thirteen	tongue	pieces
neighborhood	thousand	through	unusual	building

■ **Analogies** Write the list word that completes each analogy.

1. Bad is to good as ugly is to **beautiful** .
2. Twig is to nest as brick is to **building** .
3. Composer is to music as poet is to **poetry** .
4. Strong is to powerful as rare is to **unusual** .

■ **Context Clues** Write the list word that best completes each sentence.

5. Marla cut six **pieces** of apple pie for her family.
6. Jesse lives in a **neighborhood** of big old houses.
7. Have you ever burned your **tongue** on a slice of pizza?
8. Viking explorers came to America a **thousand** years ago.
9. In English we read the **poetry** of Robert Frost.
10. The American flag once had **thirteen** stars.
11. Snow in September is an **unusual** sight.

STRATEGIC SPELLING: Developing Spelling Consciousness
We sometimes misspell familiar words that we shouldn't miss. Proofread the passage. Find the four misspelled words and write them correctly.

It's been six weeks since we moved here, and I guess it's not so bad. We ride our bikes throw the park every day. The flowers in the park are beutiful! I like our apartment bilding. I miss my friend Shannon, but she said she would come visit when I turn thirteen.

12. **through** _____   14. **building** _____
13. **beautiful** _____   15. **thirteen** _____

8

EXTRA PRACTICE ■ 1

Word List				
poetry	beautiful	thirteen	tongue	pieces
neighborhood	thousand	through	unusual	building
license	remodel	grateful	enemy	instrument
perform	prefer	judged	adjusted	soldier

■ **Word Math** Answer each problem with a list word.

1. streets + house + people = ___
2. driver + legal + document = ___
3. rhyme + verse + similes = ___
4. vase + drop + shatter = ___
5. mouth + talk + taste = ___
6. tune + practice + music = ___
7. ten + two + one = ___
8. act + dance + sing = ___
9. weird + strange + uncommon = ___
10. contest + entrants + selected = ___
11. war + uniform + army = ___
12. finished + done + completed = ___

1. **neighborhood**
2. **license**
3. **poetry**
4. **pieces**
5. **tongue**
6. **instrument**
7. **thirteen**
8. **perform**
9. **unusual**
10. **judged**
11. **soldier**
12. **through**
13. **thousand**
14. **grateful**
15. **adjusted**
16. **beautiful**
17. **enemy**
18. **prefer**
19. **remodel**
20. **building**

■ **Riddles** Write a list word to match each clue. HINT: Use the sentence meaning and the underlined words as clues.

13. There are many, many grains of sand.
14. I'm so glad I ate before the game.
15. We just fixed the picture on the TV set.
16. Today we will be at the spectacular art show.
17. My former friend is not welcome here.
18. I will refer you to another doctor if you wish.
19. We will use this model when we restore the house.
20. The din from the construction site was deafening.

9

1 ■ REVIEW

Word List				
poetry	beautiful	thirteen	tongue	pieces
neighborhood	thousand	through	unusual	building
license	remodel	grateful	enemy	instrument
perform	prefer	judged	adjusted	soldier

■ **Antonyms** Write the list word that completes each phrase.

1. not around, but ___
2. not friend, but ___
3. not dislike, but ___
4. not ugly, but ___

■ **Associations** Write the list word that is associated with each word below.

5. act
6. teenager
7. roof
8. driving
9. war
10. orchestra
11. puzzle
12. taste

■ **Classifying** Write the list word that belongs in each group.

13. redo, rebuild, ___
14. aligned, reset, ___
15. rhyme, verse, ___
16. ten, hundred, ___

■ **Words in Context** Complete the sentence with words from the box.

judged	grateful
neighborhood	unusual

The (17) defendant was relieved when the jury (18) that she was innocent of any wrongdoing in the (19) traffic accident that happened in the (20) of the school.

1. **through**
2. **enemy**
3. **prefer**
4. **beautiful**
5. **perform**
6. **thirteen**
7. **building**
8. **license**
9. **soldier**
10. **instrument**
11. **pieces**
12. **tongue**
13. **remodel**
14. **adjusted**
15. **poetry**
16. **thousand**
17. **grateful**
18. **judged**
19. **unusual**
20. **neighborhood**

10

CHALLENGE ■ 2

Challenge Words

| adequate | reconcile | insulation | thunderstorm | reluctant |

■ Use Challenge Words to complete the relationships described below.

1. Lining is to coat as **insulation** is to house.
2. Blizzard is to snowfall as **thunderstorm** is to rain shower.
3. Delicious is to good-tasting as **adequate** is to good enough.
4. Estrange is to **reconcile** as fight is to make up.
5. Unwilling is to **reluctant** as eager is to expectant.

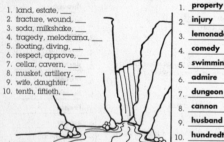

■ Did you ever try fixing something? Sometimes it's easy; sometimes it's impossible. Use Challenge Words to write a paragraph about the frustration or satisfaction of doing repairs on your own.

_____
_____
_____
_____
_____
_____
_____
_____

---

2 ■ THINK AND PRACTICE

| admire | canyon | lemonade | method | distance |
| swimming | modern | comedy | husband | clumsy |

■ **Antonyms** Write the list word that means the opposite of each word.

1. old-fashioned **modern**
2. tragedy **comedy**
3. dislike **admire**
4. graceful **clumsy**

■ **Analogies** Write the list word that completes each analogy.

5. *Woman* is to *wife* as *man* is to **husband**
6. *Track* is to *running* as *pool* is to **swimming**
7. *Oranges* are to *orange juice* as *lemons* are to **lemonade**
8. *High* is to *mountain* as *deep* is to **canyon**
9. *Quart* is to *volume* as *mile* is to **distance**
10. *Cry* is to *tragedy* as *laugh* is to **comedy**
11. *Magical* is to *magic* as *methodical* is to **method**
12. *Deer* is to *graceful* as *bull* is to **clumsy**

STRATEGIC SPELLING: Seeing Meaning Connections
Complete each sentence with a word from the box.

| Words related to *admire* | | |
| admirable | admiration | admirer |

13. William is a great **admirer** of Jackie Joyner-Kersee.
14. He thinks her athletic skills are **admirable**.
15. William expressed his **admiration** in a letter.

EXTRA PRACTICE ■ 2

Word List

admire	canyon	lemonade	method	distance
swimming	modern	comedy	husband	clumsy
magnify	cannon	decorate	strict	injury
tissue	honesty	property	hundredth	dungeon

■ **Classifying** Write the list word that belongs in each group below.

1. land, estate, ___   1. **property**
2. fracture, wound, ___   2. **injury**
3. soda, milkshake, ___   3. **lemonade**
4. tragedy, melodrama, ___   4. **comedy**
5. floating, diving, ___   5. **swimming**
6. respect, approve, ___   6. **admire**
7. cellar, cavern, ___   7. **dungeon**
8. musket, artillery, ___   8. **cannon**
9. wife, daughter, ___   9. **husband**
10. tenth, fiftieth, ___   10. **hundredth**

■ **Words in Context** Write a list word to complete each sentence.

11. Which **method** do you use to study for tests?
12. The runner ran the entire **distance** in one hour.
13. Sal felt **clumsy** when he kept tripping on his laces.
14. Can you help me **decorate** the gym for the dance?
15. Maya's mother is very **strict** about Maya's homework.
16. Dinosaurs are extinct in the **modern** world.
17. Rescuers brought the injured hiker up out of the **canyon**.
18. Carlos took off his stage makeup with a **tissue**.
19. Use the lens to **magnify** this small writing.
20. Jake's principles include **honesty** and loyalty.

---

2 ■ REVIEW

Word List

admire	canyon	lemonade	method	distance
swimming	modern	comedy	husband	clumsy
magnify	cannon	decorate	strict	injury
tissue	honesty	property	hundredth	dungeon

■ **Definitions** Write the list word that fits each definition.

1. underground prison   1. **dungeon**
2. way of doing something   2. **method**
3. policy of telling the truth 3. **honesty**
4. used after a sneeze   4. **tissue**
5. make fancy   5. **decorate**
6. increase in size   6. **magnify**
7. a funny show   7. **comedy**
8. look up to   8. **admire**
9. person married to a wife   9. **husband**

■ **Classifying** Write the list word that belongs in each group.

10. wound, trauma, ___   10. **injury**
11. tenth, ___, thousandth   11. **hundredth**
12. floating, diving, ___   12. **swimming**
13. new, innovative, ___   13. **modern**
14. limeade, orangeade, ___   14. **lemonade**
15. awkward, gawky, ___   15. **clumsy**
16. harsh, severe, ___   16. **strict**
17. valley, gorge, ___   17. **canyon**
18. far, away, ___   18. **distance**
19. gun, artillery, ___   19. **cannon**
20. possession, ownership, ___ 20. **property**

Name _____

CHALLENGE ■ 3

Challenge Words

| deceitful | retrieval | conceivable | unwieldy | grievance |

■ Write a Challenge Word to complete each equation.

1. take back + act of doing something = **retrieval**
2. not + easily managed = **unwieldy**
3. lies + filled with = **deceitful**
4. understand + able to = **conceivable**
5. mourn + action or quality of = **grievance**

■ Friends and neighbors can get into some ridiculous disagreements. Use one or more Challenge Words to write a newspaper article about a real or imagined disagreement.

_____
_____
_____
_____
_____
_____
_____
_____
_____

15

Name _____

3 ■ THINK AND PRACTICE

| ceiling | receipt | deceive | neither | field |
| achieve | belief | brief | relief | apiece |

■ **Synonyms** Write a list word that means the same as the underlined word.

1. The children flew their kites in a big meadow. **field**
2. The roses cost one dollar each. **apiece**
3. Paula's campaign speech was very short. **brief**
4. Juan is very nice. Don't let his harsh manner fool you. **deceive**
5. Mr. Wood has a strong idea that there is life on Mars. **belief**

■ **Context Clues** Write the list word that completes each sentence.

6. Noriko gave the man a **receipt** for the doll he bought.
7. **Neither** Tim nor Rob tried out for the basketball team.
8. A rain shower brought **relief** from the summer heat.
9. A college education will help you **achieve** your goals.
10. Cara hung a piñata from the **ceiling** of her room.
11. The farmer planted corn in his **field**.

STRATEGIC SPELLING: Using the Problem Parts Strategy
Write four list words that are hard for you. Underline the part of each word that gives you problems. Picture the words. Focus on the problem parts.

12. **Answers will vary.** 14. _____
13. _____ 15. _____

16

Name _____

EXTRA PRACTICE ■ 3

Word List

ceiling	receipt	deceive	neither	field
achieve	belief	brief	relief	apiece
leisure	protein	receiver	seize	conceited
shield	niece	diesel	grief	yield

■ **Long e** Write the list word that fits each clue below. HINT: All the list words in each group should rhyme with one another.

1. a strong conviction about something
2. extreme sadness
3. not lasting very long
4. something that removes pain
5. a plot of open land
6. to protect someone from something
7. to give way
8. each; for each one
9. the daughter of one's brother or sister
10. to fool or mislead
11. to reach one's goal

1. **belief**
2. **grief**
3. **brief**
4. **relief**
5. **field**
6. **shield**
7. **yield**
8. **apiece**
9. **niece**
10. **deceive**
11. **achieve**

■ **Puzzle** Use the printed letters as clues and write a list word in each set of blanks.

12. r e c e i v e r
13. c o n c e i t e d
14. s e i z e
15. d i e s e l
16. p r o t e i n
17. n e i t h e r
18. r e c e i p t
19. l e i s u r e
20. c e i l i n g

17

Name _____

3 ■ REVIEW

Word List

ceiling	receipt	deceive	neither	field
achieve	belief	brief	relief	apiece
leisure	protein	receiver	seize	conceited
shield	niece	diesel	grief	yield

■ **Pronunciations** Write a list word for each pronunciation.

1. (ə chēv′) ___
2. (kən sē′tid) ___
3. (ri sē′vər) ___

■ **Making Associations** Write the list word that is associated with each item below.

4. nephew 9. armor
5. nor 10. payment
6. engine 11. stop
7. help 12. wheat
8. vacation

■ **Antonyms** Write the list words that mean the opposite of the underlined words.

13. The floor needed repair.
14. The Smiths are enjoying a long stay at the beach.
15. Happiness overcame Joyce when she heard the unexpected news.
16. His partners tried to tell him honestly about his rights.
17. Dad decided to let go of the ball.

■ **Seeing Meaning Connections** Write the unused list words that fit the definitions.

18. for every one
19. something people accept and trust in
20. a nutritious substance found in foods

1. **achieve**
2. **conceited**
3. **receiver**
4. **niece**
5. **neither**
6. **diesel**
7. **relief**
8. **leisure**
9. **shield**
10. **receipt**
11. **yield**
12. **field**
13. **ceiling**
14. **brief**
15. **Grief**
16. **deceive**
17. **seize**
18. **apiece**
19. **belief**
20. **protein**

18

Everyday Spelling © Scott Foresman • Addison Wesley

143

CHALLENGE ■ 4

Challenge Words				
curlicue	newcomer	aptitude	ukulele	fugitive

■ Write the Challenge Word that fits each clue listed below.

1. You might find this on someone's writing. **curlicue**
2. You might find this at a folk music concert. **ukulele**
3. You might find one on the first day of school. **newcomer**
4. You might find this in yourself when you try something new. **aptitude**
5. You might find one hiding aboard a ship. **fugitive**

■ Do you dream about solving an international mystery? Use one or more Challenge Words to write a paragraph about a very important detective assignment.

_____

_____

_____

_____

_____

_____

_____

_____

_____

_____

_____

19

---

4 ■ THINK AND PRACTICE

reduce	attitude	sewer	New York	review
value	continue	humid	United States	universe

■ **Context Quotes** Write the list word that is missing from each person's statement.

1. Teacher: "The best students have a positive **attitude** ."
2. Weather forecaster: "The first day of summer will be hot and **humid** ."
3. Art dealer: "This painting will increase in **value** ."
4. Astronomer: "There are many galaxies in the **universe** ."
5. Movie critic: "I often **review** children's movies."

■ **Classifying** Write the word that belongs in each group.

6. drainage, gutter, **sewer**
7. advance, move ahead, **continue**
8. France, China, **United States**
9. lessen, decrease, **reduce**
10. Texas, California, **New York**
11. sticky, muggy, **humid**

STRATEGIC SPELLING: Seeing Meaning Connections
Write words from the box that fit the definitions.

Words with *view*			
review	viewpoint	preview	interview

12. A meeting at which a reporter gets information is an **interview** .
13. An advance showing of a movie is a **preview** .
14. A standpoint on a subject is a **viewpoint** .
15. An evaluation of a book or a play is a **review** .

20

EXTRA PRACTICE ■ 4

Word List				
reduce	attitude	sewer	New York	review
value	continue	humid	United States	universe
costume	absolutely	assume	renew	viewpoint
interview	preview	rescue	uniform	reunion

■ **Words in Context** Write the list word that is missing from each person's statement.

1. Diet Expert: "If you ___ you will be healthier." — 1. **reduce**
2. Magazine Seller: "Would you like to ___ your subscription?" — 2. **renew**
3. News Reporter: "My ___ with the president went well." — 3. **interview**
4. Politician: "I will ___ not raise your taxes!" — 4. **absolutely**
5. Nurse: "My new ___ has a button missing." — 5. **uniform**
6. Moviegoer: "I hope they show a ___ of the new science fiction show." — 6. **preview**
7. Writer: "My character lives beneath ___ City." — 7. **New York**
8. Debate Coach: "Be sure to state your ___ clearly." — 8. **viewpoint**
9. Newspaper Reader: "I disagree with this movie ___!" — 9. **review**
10. Principal: "The class of '47 will hold their ___ next weekend." — 10. **reunion**
11. Tour Director: "We'll fly across the ___ to California." — 11. **United States**
12. Astronomer: "The ___ is larger than we can imagine!" — 12. **universe**

■ **Base Words** Write the list word that is the base word for each word below.

13. attitudes — 13. **attitude**
14. continued — 14. **continue**
15. rescuer — 15. **rescue**
16. costuming — 16. **costume**
17. assuming — 17. **assume**
18. valuable — 18. **value**
19. sewers — 19. **sewer**
20. humidity — 20. **humid**

21

---

4 ■ REVIEW

Word List				
reduce	attitude	sewer	New York	review
value	continue	humid	United States	universe
costume	absolutely	assume	renew	viewpoint
interview	preview	rescue	uniform	reunion

■ **Base Words** Write the list word that is the base word of each word below.

1. rescued — 1. **rescue**
2. uniformity — 2. **uniform**
3. humidify — 3. **humid**
4. continuous — 4. **continue**
5. universal — 5. **universe**
6. renewal — 6. **renew**
7. valuable — 7. **value**
8. assuming — 8. **assume**
9. reducible — 9. **reduce**

■ **Analogies** Write the list word that completes each analogy.

10. Paper is to trash can as water is to ___. — 10. **sewer**
11. Play is to critique as book is to ___. — 11. **review**
12. Family is to gathering as student is to ___. — 12. **reunion**
13. Painter is to coveralls as actor is to ___. — 13. **costume**
14. Windy City is to Chicago as Big Apple is to ___. — 14. **New York**
15. Sample is to food as ___ is to movie. — 15. **preview**
16. Europe is to France as America is to ___. — 16. **United States**
17. Sincerely is to wholeheartedly as completely is to ___. — 17. **absolutely**

■ **Exact Meanings** Write the list word that makes sense in each sentence below.

18. All the reporters were on hand to ___ the mayor. — 18. **interview**
19. Success has a lot to do with having a positive ___. — 19. **attitude**
20. The book was written from the author's ___. — 20. **viewpoint**

22

Name ______________________

CHALLENGE ■ 5

Challenge Words

patrolled, patrolling, dignified, dignifying, staggered, staggering

■ Complete the following police report using the correct forms of the Challenge Words.

I was **patrolling** a neighborhood I had often **patrolled** before, when a **dignified** old woman **staggered** out of a doorway and down the street. She was carrying a heavy object. I called out to ask whether she needed help, but she was not **dignifying** my silly question with an answer. So I walked over to help her. I was shocked to see her stop **staggering** and start to sprint away! She was none other than Galloping Gabby, that white-haired Robin Hood of the city.

■ Imagine that Galloping Gabby got caught. Write a paragraph about the scene above from her point of view. Use one or more Challenge Words in your description.

____

____

____

____

____

____

____

____

____

____

Name ______________________

5 ■ THINK AND PRACTICE

answered	answering	decided	deciding	included
including	omitted	omitting	satisfied	satisfying

■ **Complete a Paragraph** Write a list word to complete each sentence in the paragraph.

Rolanda was (1) **deciding** which sport to play after school. She wrote down her choices, which (2) **included** soccer and basketball. When her teacher asked which sport she had chosen, she (3) **answered** that she wasn't sure. Then she realized she had (4) **omitted** one sport. Rolanda got her racket and ran to the tennis court, feeling (5) **satisfied** with her choice.

■ **Adding Endings** Write the list words formed by adding **-ed** or **-ing.**

6. decide + ed **decided**
7. omit + ing **omitting**
8. answer + ing **answering**
9. satisfy + ing **satisfying**
10. include + ing **including**

STRATEGIC SPELLING: Building New Words

Add **-ed** and **-ing** to each of these words: *prefer, license, magnify, continue,* and *shield.* Remember what you learned.

	Add -ed	Add -ing
11.	preferred	preferring
12.	licensed	licensing
13.	magnified	magnifying
14.	continued	continuing
15.	shielded	shielding

Name ______________________

EXTRA PRACTICE ■ 5

Word List

answered	answering	decided	deciding	included
including	omitted	omitting	satisfied	satisfying
delayed	delaying	remembered	remembering	exercised
exercising	interfered	interfering	occurred	occurring

■ **Word Forms** Write the list word that makes sense in each sentence and has the same ending as the underlined word.

1. Dieting and ___ often go together.
2. The explosions kept ___ and frightening the town.
3. Our flight was ___ and rerouted because of the storm.
4. That store always has pleased and ___ customers.
5. No one ___ the phone when I called.
6. Grandma was ___ old times and laughing about them.
7. We are packing and ___ several days' clothing.
8. We discussed the test and ___ to study together.
9. The pounding annoyed me and ___ with my sleep.
10. When Nan looked at the empty envelope, she saw that she had ___ the card.

■ **What's Missing?** Write the list word to complete each group below.

11. delay, delayed, ___
12. answer, answered, ___
13. remember, remembering, ___
14. interfere, interfered, ___
15. decide, decided, ___
16. include, including, ___
17. exercise, exercising, ___
18. omit, omitted, ___
19. occur, occurring, ___
20. satisfy, satisfied, ___

1. **exercising**
2. **occurring**
3. **delayed**
4. **satisfied**
5. **answered**
6. **remembering**
7. **including**
8. **decided**
9. **interfered**
10. **omitted**
11. **delaying**
12. **answering**
13. **remembered**
14. **interfering**
15. **deciding**
16. **included**
17. **exercised**
18. **omitting**
19. **occurred**
20. **satisfying**

Name ______________________

5 ■ REVIEW

Word List

answered	answering	decided	deciding	included
including	omitted	omitting	satisfied	satisfying
delayed	delaying	remembered	remembering	exercised
exercising	interfered	interfering	occurred	occurring

■ **Double Duty** Add two suffixes to each word in parentheses to form list words that complete each sentence.

1–2. (satisfy) To have ___ guests, serve ___ meals.

3–4. (omit) Joe wished he had ___ the salt instead of ___ the cinnamon.

5–6. (exercise) The more they ___, the more they loved ___.

■ **Words That Add Up** Write the list word that has each meaning and ending given below.

7. reply + ed = ___
8. hesitation + ing = ___
9. contain + ed = ___
10. meddle + ing = ___
11. recall + ing = ___
12. happen + ed = ___
13. conclude + ing = ___

■ **Classifying** Write the list word that is most similar in meaning to each word or phrase below.

14. reminisced
15. butted in
16. postponed
17. taking place
18. responding
19. involving
20. determined

1. **satisfied**
2. **satisfying**
3. **omitted**
4. **omitting**
5. **exercised**
6. **exercising**
7. **answered**
8. **delaying**
9. **included**
10. **interfering**
11. **remembering**
12. **occurred**
13. **deciding**
14. **remembered**
15. **interfered**
16. **delayed**
17. **occurring**
18. **answering**
19. **including**
20. **decided**

REVIEW ■ 6A

Lesson 1

poetry	thirteen	tongue	neighborhood	building

■ **Associations** Write the list word that is associated with each item.

1. rhymes   **poetry**
2. skyscraper   **building**
3. taste   **tongue**
4. number   **thirteen**
5. houses   **neighborhood**

Lesson 2

canyon	method	swimming	comedy	husband

■ **Definitions** Write the list word that is missing from each person's statement.

1. Explorer: "I will hike through this rocky **canyon** ."
2. Athlete: "Today I will practice **swimming** laps."
3. Wife: "I will call my **husband** ."
4. Scientist: "What scientific **method** will I use in this experiment?"
5. Actor: "My next movie is a **comedy** ."

Lesson 3

achieve	field	relief	receipt	deceive

■ **Making Connections** Write the list word that answers each question.

1. What do you get to show you have paid?   **receipt**
2. What might a fan give you on a hot day?   **relief**
3. What do people who are not honest do?   **deceive**
4. Where does a farmer plant crops?   **field**
5. What do you do when you accomplish something?   **achieve**

27

6B ■ REVIEW

Lesson 4

reduce	New York	review	continue	United States

■ **Drawing Conclusions** Write the list word that matches each clue.

1. a large city   **New York**
2. a country with fifty states   **United States**
3. to go on   **continue**
4. the opposite of *preview*   **review**
5. a synonym for *decrease*   **reduce**

Lesson 5

answered	deciding	including	satisfied	omitting

■ **Word Forms** For each base word, write the **-ed** or **-ing** form.

Base word	-ed	-ing
1. answer	**answered**	answering
2. omit	omitted	**omitting**
3. satisfy	**satisfied**	satisfying
4. include	included	**including**
5. decide	decided	**deciding**

28

Name _____

CHALLENGE ■ 7

Challenge Words		
martial	marshall	bizarre
bazaar	discreet	discrete

■ Answer the clues below to complete each of the puzzles.

```
m a r s h a l l
a
r       b i z a r r e
t       a
i       z           d i s c r e e t
a       a           i
l       a           s
        r           c
                    r
                    e
                    t
                    e
```

Across
1. an official
2. very strange
3. respectful, reserved

Down
1. about war
2. outdoor market
3. separate

■ Travel, whether by plane, car, or imagination, can be exciting. Use one or more Challenge Words to write a paragraph about an exotic place you have visited or read about.

_____

_____

_____

_____

_____

_____

29

Name _____

7 ■ THINK AND PRACTICE

their	there	they're	wring	ring
chili	chilly	scent	sent	cent

■ **Definitions** Read each sentence. Write the correct word for each definition.

A chilly fall evening is a good time to eat chili.

cool	a spicy stew
1. chilly	2. chili

Theresa's mom sent her a bouquet with a sweet scent.

fragrance	had delivered
3. scent	4. sent

They're practicing free throws over there.

in that place	they are
5. there	6. they're

■ **Word Choice** Write the correct list word for each sentence.

7. (Ring, Wring) out your swimsuit after you swim. — Wring
8. They planted corn in (their, they're) backyard. — their
9. Kelly (sent, cent) us a postcard from camp. — sent
10. Akiko found a golden (wring, ring) in the park. — ring
11. What can you buy with one (sent, cent)? — cent
12. Nights are (chilly, chili) in the desert. — chilly

STRATEGIC SPELLING: Using the Memory Tricks Strategy
Use memory tricks to help you use homophones correctly. Create homophone sentences for each pair or triplet.

13. chili—chilly — Answers will vary.
14. scent—sent—cent — Answers will vary.
15. their—there—they're — Answers will vary.

30

Name _____

EXTRA PRACTICE ■ 7

Word List				
their	there	they're	wring	ring
chili	chilly	scent	sent	cent
oversees	overseas	patients	patience	cereal
serial	coarse	course	counsel	council

■ **Which Is It?** Use homophones to complete each question-and-answer pair below.

1. Is that new western ___ on TV any good?
2. Yes, except for all the silly ___ commercials.
3. Who is the person who ___ your factories in Asia?
4. Mr. Ray deals with our ___ operations.
5. Would you like a cold drink with your ___?
6. Thanks, but I'm too ___ for that.
7. Why do you have all this ___ wool?
8. I'm taking a ___ in how to make wall hangings.
9. Has the student ___ made a decision yet?
10. No, they're seeking ___ from Ms. Travis first.
11. How many ___ did you see today, Doctor?
12. After about forty, I ran out of ___!
13. Would you ___ out these wet towels?
14. Sure, but let me take my ___ off, first.

1. serial
2. cereal
3. oversees
4. overseas
5. chili
6. chilly
7. coarse
8. course
9. council
10. counsel
11. patients
12. patience
13. wring
14. ring

■ **Making Inferences** Use homophones to fit the clues below.

15. This helps you pay the bus driver.
16. This is what you did when you mailed a letter.
17. This tells your nose what's for dinner.
18. This word usually makes you think of *where*.
19. This word combines a pronoun and a verb.
20. This tells about belonging to someone.

15. cent
16. sent
17. scent
18. there
19. they're
20. their

31

Name _____

7 ■ REVIEW

Word List				
their	there	they're	wring	ring
chili	chilly	scent	sent	cent
oversees	overseas	patients	patience	cereal
serial	coarse	course	counsel	council

■ **Making Connections** Write a list word that fits the clues below.

1. This food is peppery hot.
2. A manager does this.
3. Doctors take care of these.
4. This is one penny.
5. Get water out of cloth this way.
6. This is where Africa is.
7. Bloodhounds sniff for this.
8. This describes one type of sandpaper.
9. This might crackle when you add milk.
10. This is done to letters.
11. When you're upset, you run out of this.

1. chili
2. oversees
3. patients
4. cent
5. wring
6. overseas
7. scent
8. coarse
9. cereal
10. sent
11. patience

■ **Exact Meanings** Write the list word that makes sense in each sentence below.

12. It's a snowy, ___ night outside.
13–14. Of ___ you may have another serving, but I would ___ against it.
15. That newspaper story is a ___, with an episode every Friday.
16. Did someone ___ the doorbell?
17. The ___ voted for a new playground.

12. chilly
13. course
14. counsel
15. serial
16. ring
17. council

■ **Triple Homophones** Complete the paragraph below with three list words that sound alike.

Over (18) are the Puli puppies I told you about, the ones whose hair grows into a mop of coiled ropes. Originally, these intelligent dogs came from Hungary, and (19) great watchdogs for (20) owners.

18. there
19. they're
20. their

32

147

CHALLENGE ■ 8

Challenge Words				
discipline	indebtedness	monologue	misguided	susceptible

■ Write a Challenge Word to complete each equation.

1. training + obedience = **discipline**
2. wrong + led = **misguided**
3. owing + a state of = **indebtedness**
4. single + talk = **monologue**
5. sensitive + able = **susceptible**

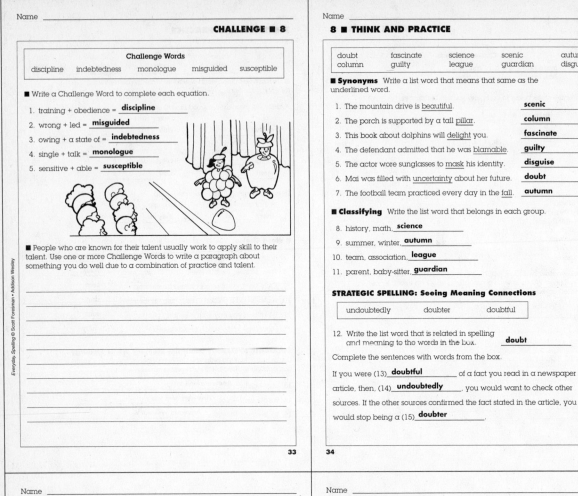

■ People who are known for their talent usually work to apply skill to their talent. Use one or more Challenge Words to write a paragraph about something you do well due to a combination of practice and talent.

_____

_____

_____

_____

_____

_____

_____

_____

_____

33

---

8 ■ THINK AND PRACTICE

doubt	fascinate	science	scenic	autumn
column	guilty	league	guardian	disguise

■ **Synonyms** Write a list word that means that same as the underlined word.

1. The mountain drive is beautiful. **scenic**
2. The porch is supported by a tall pillar. **column**
3. This book about dolphins will delight you. **fascinate**
4. The defendant admitted that he was blamable. **guilty**
5. The actor wore sunglasses to mask his identity. **disguise**
6. Mai was filled with uncertainty about her future. **doubt**
7. The football team practiced every day in the fall. **autumn**

■ **Classifying** Write the list word that belongs in each group.

8. history, math. **science**
9. summer, winter. **autumn**
10. team, association. **league**
11. parent, baby-sitter. **guardian**

STRATEGIC SPELLING: Seeing Meaning Connections

undoubtedly	doubter	doubtful

12. Write the list word that is related in spelling and meaning to the words in the box. **doubt**

Complete the sentences with words from the box.

If you were (13) **doubtful** of a fact you read in a newspaper article, then, (14) **undoubtedly** , you would want to check other sources. If the other sources confirmed the fact stated in the article, you would stop being a (15) **doubter** .

34

EXTRA PRACTICE ■ 8

Word List				
doubt	fascinate	science	scenic	autumn
column	guilty	league	guardian	disguise
subtle	debt	reminiscent	descend	condemn
solemn	guidance	vague	fatigue	intrigue

■ **Synonyms** Write the list word that means the same as each word below.

1. protector
2. convicted
3. weariness
4. serious
5. camouflage
6. unclear
7. mystery
8. picturesque
9. advice
10. recalling

1. **guardian**
2. **guilty**
3. **fatigue**
4. **solemn**
5. **disguise**
6. **vague**
7. **intrigue**
8. **scenic**
9. **guidance**
10. **reminiscent**

■ **Base Words** Write the list word that is the base word for each word below.

11. doubtful
12. condemns
13. fascinating
14. scientific
15. columns
16. subtly
17. descendant
18. leagues
19. debtor
20. autumnal

11. **doubt**
12. **condemn**
13. **fascinate**
14. **science**
15. **column**
16. **subtle**
17. **descend**
18. **league**
19. **debt**
20. **autumn**

35

---

8 ■ REVIEW

Word List				
doubt	fascinate	science	scenic	autumn
column	guilty	league	guardian	disguise
subtle	debt	reminiscent	descend	condemn
solemn	guidance	vague	fatigue	intrigue

■ **Synonyms** Write a list word that means the same as each word below.

1. gentle   5. conspiracy
2. tire   6. row
3. question   7. hazy
4. spellbind   8. serious

1. **subtle**
2. **fatigue**
3. **doubt**
4. **fascinate**
5. **intrigue**
6. **column**
7. **vague**
8. **solemn**

■ **Context Clues** Write the list word that best completes each sentence.

9. The jury found the thief ___ as charged.
10. We decided to take the ___ route along the mountain ridge.
11. Jan's doctor bills put her family in ___.
12. Peter Pan was able to ___ to the stage on an invisible rope.
13. Counselors provide ___.
14. Colorful leaves are the prettiest ___ fashions of all.
15. That perfume is faintly ___ of one my grandmother wore.

9. **guilty**
10. **scenic**
11. **debt**
12. **descend**
13. **guidance**
14. **autumn**
15. **reminiscent**

■ **Proofreading** Find the misspelled word in each sentence and write it correctly.

16. The judge chose to condemn the criminal's behavior.
17. Jane wants to be the first female player in the leaque.
18. Math and sciance are their best subjects.
19. We recognized Harold despite his disguise.
20. Fairy tales are full of gardien angels.

16. **condemn**
17. **league**
18. **science**
19. **disguise**
20. **guardian**

36

Name _____

CHALLENGE ■ 9

Challenge Words		
embarrassment	dilemma	unnecessarily
compassionately	accompaniment	

■ Use Challenge Words to solve the clues and complete the crossword puzzle.

Across
1. with concern for another
5. troubling problem

Down
2. something added to the basics
3. a flustered feeling
4. needlessly

Crossword answers: compassionately (across), dilemma, accompaniment, unnecessarily, embarrassment

■ Everyone gets into a difficult situation now and then. Use one or more Challenge Words to write a paragraph about helping someone—or being helped—out of a difficult situation.

_____
_____
_____
_____
_____

37

Name _____

9 ■ THINK AND PRACTICE

connect	command	mirror	accomplish	according
allowance	college	address	Mississippi	recess

■ **Analogies** Write the list word that completes each analogy.

1. Teacher is to school as professor is to **college**
2. Hostess is to invite as king is to **command**
3. View is to window as reflection is to **mirror**
4. Richmond is to Virginia as Jackson is to **Mississippi**
5. Study is to class as play is to **recess**
6. Seem is to seeming as accord is to **according**

■ **Associations** Write the list word that is associated with each item.

7. telephone number — **address**
8. unite — **connect**
9. makeup — **mirror**
10. achieve — **accomplish**
11. playground — **recess**
12. chores — **allowance**
13. river — **Mississippi**

STRATEGIC SPELLING: Using the Memory Tricks Strategy
Use memory tricks to help you spell. Choose two list words that are difficult for you. Identify the parts of these words that give you problems. Then create memory tricks for those words. Underline the matching letters in the list words and helpers.

14. **Answers will vary.**
_____

15. **Answers will vary.**
_____

38

Name _____

EXTRA PRACTICE ■ 9

Word List				
connect	command	mirror	accomplish	according
allowance	college	address	Mississippi	recess
committee	immediate	barricade	interrupt	broccoli
collect	afford	possess	Tennessee	announce

■ **Word Math** Write the list word that completes each equation.

1. green + vitamins + vegetable = ___
2. money + regular + child = ___
3. gate + closed + railroad tracks = ___
4. street + house + number = ___
5. glass + reflect + face = ___
6. group + meeting + discuss = ___
7. microphone + information + speaker = ___
8. study + dorm + degree = ___
9. try + succeed + proud = ___
10. river + Mark Twain + flood = ___

1. **broccoli**
2. **allowance**
3. **barricade**
4. **address**
5. **mirror**
6. **committee**
7. **announce**
8. **college**
9. **accomplish**
10. **Mississippi**

■ **Double Clues** The list words in this lesson all contain double consonants. Use the clues to write list words.

11. Two **m's** give you something right this minute.
12. Two pairs of **s's** means you own it.
13. Two **l's** lets you gather up all your baseball cards.
14. Two **f's** means you have enough money to buy.
15. Two **n's** and two **s's** give you a southern state.
16. Two **r's** is what you do when you break into someone else's conversation.
17. Two **n's** means to join things together.
18. Two **m's** is an order.
19. Two **s's** is a break in the school day.
20. Two **c's** with the word to means "based on."

11. **immediate**
12. **possess**
13. **collect**
14. **afford**
15. **Tennessee**
16. **interrupt**
17. **connect**
18. **command**
19. **recess**
20. **according**

39

Name _____

9 ■ REVIEW

Word List				
connect	command	mirror	accomplish	according
allowance	college	address	Mississippi	recess
committee	immediate	barricade	interrupt	broccoli
collect	afford	possess	Tennessee	announce

■ **Hidden Words** Each word below is hidden in a list word. Write the list word.

1. dress
2. low
3. see
4. and
5. for
6. cord
7. ounce
8. sip
9. up
10. mitt
11. leg
12. media

1. **address**
2. **allowance**
3. **Tennessee**
4. **command**
5. **afford**
6. **according**
7. **announce**
8. **Mississippi**
9. **interrupt**
10. **committee**
11. **college**
12. **immediate**

■ **Synonyms in Context** Write a list word that means about the same as the underlined word or words in each sentence.

13. Who's going to gather answer sheets?
14. I didn't associate the two incidents.
15. Did the spies manage to carry off their mission?
16. There was a blockade around the burning house.
17. The children are outside for play period.

13. **collect**
14. **connect**
15. **accomplish**
16. **barricade**
17. **recess**

■ **Words in Context** Write the list word that could be used to complete each phrase below.

18. ___ on the wall
19. ___ in the salad
20. ___ things

18. **mirror**
19. **broccoli**
20. **possess**

40

149

Everyday Spelling © Scott Foresman • Addison Wesley

CHALLENGE ■ 10

Challenge Words

New Year's Eve	millionaire's	millionaires'
roommate's	roommates'	

■ Complete the following sentences with the correct Challenge Word.

1. The __millionaires'__ yacht belonged to a group of twelve people.
2. The __millionaire's__ yacht was her pride and joy.
3. The last night of the year is __New Year's Eve__.
4. The __roommates'__ bookshelves were things they shared.
5. Her __roommate's__ book is on the top shelf.

■ People like to read or think about fantastic adventures. Write an adventure story that uses intriguing details and fantastic events. Use one or more Challenge Words.

_____

_____

_____

_____

_____

_____

_____

_____

_____

_____

_____

41

---

10 ■ THINK AND PRACTICE

it's	let's	that's	we'd	don't
there's	coach's	coaches'	man's	men's

■ **Possessives** Write the correct list word for each sentence.

1. The basketball (coaches', coach's) wife came to every game.
   __coach's__
2. The (men's, man's) locker room was crowded before the swim meet.
   __men's__
3. That (man's, men's) dog is well-behaved. __man's__
4. Both (coach's, coaches') suggestions were considered by the players.
   __coaches'__

■ **Contractions** Write the contraction for the underlined words in the sentences.

5. When the movie is over, let us go out for pizza. __let's__
6. I think there is a monster in the pond. __there's__
7. Why do not snakes live in Hawaii? __don't__
8. It is raining, but the sun is shining. __It's__
9. We had never seen the Grand Canyon before. __We'd__
10. Mom said that is the last piece of pie. __that's__
11. Do not touch the stove while it is still hot. __it's__

STRATEGIC SPELLING: Building New Words

Add the contraction for *had* or *would* to the base words. Remember what you learned.

	Base word	Contraction with -'d
12.	I	__I'd__
13.	you	__you'd__
14.	he	__he'd__
15.	they	__they'd__

42

EXTRA PRACTICE ■ 10

Word List

it's	let's	that's	we'd	don't
there's	coach's	coaches'	man's	men's
you're	she'd	mustn't	o'clock	guide's
guides'	director's	directors'	city's	cities'

■ **Contractions** Find the words in each sentence that can be made into a contraction. Write the list word contraction.

1. There is a lock on the door.
2. The explosives must not be placed near heat.
3. At noon we had finished our test.
4. I think it is terrible to hurt animals.
5. She would like to invite you for dinner.
6. You are humming while I try to study.
7. *Star Trek* begins at seven of the clock.
8. The movie is about to begin, so let us get some popcorn.
9. That is a fine painting of Stu's mother.
10. At our house we do not have snacks before dinner."

1. __There's__
2. __mustn't__
3. __we'd__
4. __it's__
5. __She'd__
6. __You're__
7. __o'clock__
8. __let's__
9. __That's__
10. __don't__
11. __director's__
12. __city's__
13. __guides'__
14. __coaches'__
15. __directors'__
16. __men's__
17. __cities'__
18. __guide's__
19. __man's__
20. __coach's__

■ **Possessives** Write the list word that goes with each phrase below. Belonging to:

11. —the director of the play
12. —one large city
13. —two guides at a state park
14. —the coaches of a professional team
15. —several directors of a company
16. —two adult male persons
17. —more than one city
18. —the guide of a vacation tour
19. —one adult male person
20. —the coach of the volleyball team

43

---

10 ■ REVIEW

Word List

it's	let's	that's	we'd	don't
there's	coach's	coaches'	man's	men's
you're	she'd	mustn't	o'clock	guide's
guides'	director's	directors'	city's	cities'

■ **Contractions** Write the contraction that contains each word below.

1. she
2. that
3. do
4. let
5. it
6. you
7. clock
8. there
9. we
10. must

1. __she'd__
2. __that's__
3. __don't__
4. __let's__
5. __it's__
6. __you're__
7. __o'clock__
8. __there's__
9. __we'd__
10. __mustn't__
11. __men's__
12. __cities'__
13. __coaches'__
14. __directors'__
15. __guides'__
16. __coach's__
17. __guide's__
18. __city's__
19. __man's__
20. __director's__

■ **Classifying** Write the list word that belongs in each group.

11. guys', fellows', ___
12. villages', towns', ___
13. trainers', instructors', ___
14. managers', supervisors', ___
15. scouts', trackers', ___

■ **Word Forms** Write the possessive form of each word in parentheses to complete each set of words or phrase.

16. ___ (coach) conference
17. the ___ (guide) binoculars
18. the ___ (city) water system
19. the ___ (man) costume
20. ___ (director) award

44

CHALLENGE ■ 11

Challenge Words				
money order	brokenhearted	sweatshirt	turtleneck	health food

■ Put these word pairs together to create the Challenge Words.

1. cash + demand = __money order__
2. perspiration + garment = __sweatshirt__
3. shattered + organ = __brokenhearted__
4. reptile + body part = __turtleneck__
5. wellness + nourishment = __health food__

■ Have you ever lost something that you cared about? Perhaps a keepsake you treasured was lost. Write a paragraph using one or more Challenge Words to tell about it.

_____

_____

_____

_____

_____

_____

_____

_____

_____

_____

_____

_____

11 ■ THINK AND PRACTICE

myself	themselves	hallway	homeroom	everything
ice cream	locker room	tape recorder	root beer	dead end

■ **Compounds** Match a word from each column to make a list word. Write the list words.

them	beer		
home	self	1.	__themselves__
tape	selves	2.	__homeroom__
my	room	3.	__tape recorder__
root	recorder	4.	__myself__
		5.	__root beer__

■ **Joining Words** Find two words in each sentence that can be joined to make a list word. Write the word.

6. The cat found a dead bird at the end of the path. __dead end__
7. Lee put cream in the coffee and ice in the tea. __ice cream__
8. Every piece of art is a beautiful thing. __everything__
9. Stuart left his paper at home in his room. __homeroom__
10. Do you know the way to the science hall? __hallway__
11. Do you have any room in your locker? __locker room__
12. Maya put a silly thing in every person's desk. __everything__

STRATEGIC SPELLING: Seeing Meaning Connections

Words with *ice*		
iceberg	ice bag	ice pick

Write the words from the box that fit the clues.

13. a tool for chipping ice __ice pick__
14. a floating mass of ice __iceberg__
15. a container for applying ice to the body __ice bag__

EXTRA PRACTICE ■ 11

Word List				
myself	themselves	hallway	homeroom	everything
ice cream	locker room	tape recorder	root beer	dead end
teenage	teammate	skateboard	everybody	doughnut
air conditioner	polka dot	roller coaster	ice pack	solar system

■ **Classifying** Write the list word that belongs in each group below.

1. tape deck, video recorder, ___
2. ourselves, yourselves, ___
3. soda pop, ginger ale, ___
4. cupcake, gingersnap, ___
5. Milky Way, full moon, ___
6. classmate, roommate, ___
7. alleyway, pathway, ___
8. Ferris wheel, water slide, ___

1. __tape recorder__
2. __themselves__
3. __root beer__
4. __doughnut__
5. __solar system__
6. __teammate__
7. __hallway__
8. __roller coaster__

■ **Make Them Yourself** Add the missing words to form list words.

9. ___self
10. locker ___
11. home___
12. ___ cream
13. ___board
14. polka ___
15. teen___
16. ___body
17. air ___
18. ___ pack
19. ___thing
20. dead ___

9. __myself__
10. __locker room__
11. __homeroom__
12. __ice cream__
13. __skateboard__
14. __polka dot__
15. __teenage__
16. __everybody__
17. __air conditioner__
18. __ice pack__
19. __everything__
20. __dead end__

11 ■ REVIEW

Word List				
myself	themselves	hallway	homeroom	everything
ice cream	locker room	tape recorder	root beer	dead end
teenage	teammate	skateboard	everybody	doughnut
air conditioner	polka dot	roller coaster	ice pack	solar system

■ **Making Inferences** Write the list word that matches each clue.

1. Earth is one planet in this.
2. There are lots of athletes here.
3. This comes with and without jelly.
4. You'll often find a coat closet here.
5. This makes a trio with *me* and *I*.
6. Useless efforts usually end up here.
7–8. Put these white and brown things together to get a tasty soda.
9. Its power comes from your feet.

1. __solar system__
2. __locker room__
3. __doughnut__
4. __hallway__
5. __myself__
6. __dead end__
7. __ice cream__
8. __root beer__
9. __skateboard__

■ **Context Clues** Write the list word that completes each sentence.

10. Put an ___ on sprains.
11. The winners should be proud of ___.
12. The ___ broke when the temperature hit 105°F.
13. It seems like ___ is going wrong today.

10. __ice pack__
11. __themselves__
12. __air conditioner__
13. __everything__

■ **Word Match** Match the words in each column to make list words. Write the words.

14. every room
15. tape body
16. teen coaster
17. home dot
18. team recorder
19. roller age
20. polka mate

14. __everybody__
15. __tape recorder__
16. __teenage__
17. __homeroom__
18. __teammate__
19. __roller coaster__
20. __polka dot__

Name _____

Lesson 7				
wring	chili	their	scent	cent

■ **Homophones** Write the correct list word for each sentence.

1. (Wring, Ring) some of the water out of the mop.   **Wring**
2. A skunk's (cent, scent) is really strong.   **scent**
3. Do you put beans in your (chilly, chili)?   **chili**
4. When does (there, their) school play begin?   **their**
5. I spent my last (cent, sent) on stamps.   **cent**

Lesson 8				
doubt	science	autumn	league	guilty

■ **Analogies** Write the list word that completes each analogy.

1. Summer is to winter as spring is to **autumn**
2. Good is to bad as innocent is to **guilty**
3. Colleges are to university as teams are to **league**
4. Sure is to certain as uncertainty is to **doubt**
5. Ball is to sports as microscope is to **science**

Lesson 9				
recess	connect	command	college	Mississippi

■ **Classifying** Write the list word that belongs in each group.

1. join, put together, **connect**
2. Missouri, Illinois, **Mississippi**
3. break, rest, **recess**
4. preschool, junior high, **college**
5. order, edict, **command**

49

Name _____

Lesson 10				
coach's	men's	that's	we'd	don't

■ **Seeing Relationships** Write the list word that matches each clue.

1. plural possessive of *man*   **men's**
2. contraction for *that is*   **that's**
3. singular possessive of *coach*   **coach's**
4. a word using a contraction for *not*   **don't**
5. a word using a contraction for *had*   **we'd**

Lesson 11				
hallway	homeroom	ice cream	locker room	dead end

■ **Riddles** Write the list word that answers each riddle.

1. What is used to connect rooms?   **hallway**
2. What might be found in a freezer?   **ice cream**
3. Where might an athlete change clothes?   **locker room**
4. Where might a street stop?   **dead end**
5. Where might you find a student?   **homeroom**

50

CHALLENGE ■ 13

Challenge Words				
malicious	precocious	sensational	vaccination	fictitious

■ Use the Challenge Words listed above to complete these sets of opposites.

1. I thought it was a **true** story, but it turned out to be
   fictitious

2. To avoid getting **diseases,** we each got a _**vaccination**_ before our trip.

3. Last year's haunted house was **dull,** but this year's will be
   sensational

4. Once he was **kind**; now he is _**malicious**_.

5. At first, some thought she was **slow to learn** the piano, but she's really
   precocious

■ Imagine you are a reporter, and you have been assigned to tell the real story of a famous person. Use one or more Challenge Words to set the record straight.

_____
_____
_____
_____
_____
_____
_____
_____
_____
_____

51

---

13 ■ THINK AND PRACTICE

social	precious	commercial	especially	national
dictionary	motion	position	population	question

■ **Synonyms** Write the list word that means the same as each synonym.

1. action   **motion**
2. cherished   **precious**
3. inquire   **question**
4. location   **position**
5. particularly **especially**
6. ad   **commercial**

■ **Definitions** Write the list word that fits the definition.

7. a reference book about words   **dictionary**
8. an advertisement on radio or television **commercial**
9. the number of people who live in a place **population**
10. having to do with a country   **national**
11. having to do with company or companionship **social**
12. of great value   **precious**

STRATEGIC SPELLING: Using the Meaning Helpers Strategy
A meaning helper—a shorter word related in spelling and meaning—can help you spell a longer word. For example, thinking of *suggest* will help you remember the **t** in *suggestion.* Write *commercial, question,* and *population.* Write a meaning helper below each one and underline the matching letter.

13. **commercial**
    commerce
14. **question**
    quest
15. **population**
    populate

52

EXTRA PRACTICE ■ 13

Word List				
social	precious	commercial	especially	national
dictionary	motion	position	population	question
artificial	financial	gracious	glacier	suggestion
cautious	mention	fraction	exhaustion	digestion

■ **Analogies** Write a list word to complete each sentence.

1. Note is to symphony as word is to _**dictionary**_.
2. Rock is to mountain as ice is to _**glacier**_.
3. Ten is to whole number as ¼ is to _**fraction**_.
4. State is to regional as country is to _**national**_.
5. Southwest is to direction as upright is to _**position**_.
6. Certain is to uncertain as answer is to _**question**_.
7. Original is to copy as real is to _**artificial**_.
8. Sitting is to still as running is to _**motion**_.
9. Rash is to foolhardy as wary is to _**cautious**_.
10. Relate is to relation as populate is to _**population**_.
11. Gravel is to worthless as gold is to _**precious**_.
12. School is to educational as bank is to _**financial**_.

■ **Spelling Sounds** Write each remaining list word in the column that tells how /**ch**/ or /**sh**/ is spelled.

/**ch**/ spelled *ti*		/**sh**/ spelled *ci*	
13. **exhaustion**		17. **especially**	
14. **suggestion**		18. **social**	
15. **mention**		19. **gracious**	
16. **digestion**		20. **commercial**	

53

---

13 ■ REVIEW

Word List				
social	precious	commercial	especially	national
dictionary	motion	position	population	question
artificial	financial	gracious	glacier	suggestion
cautious	mention	fraction	exhaustion	digestion

■ **Word Forms** Write the list words that contain the base words below.

1. suggest
2. finance
3. special
4. digest
5. commerce
6. exhaust

■ **Antonyms** Write the list word that means the opposite of each word below.

7. carefree
8. whole
9. omit
10. real
11. answer

■ **Word Addition** Write the list word that has each meaning and ending listed below.

12. place + ion
13. people + ion
14. country + al
15. words + definitions + ary
16. ice + mountain + ier
17. get together + al
18. valuable + ous
19. move + ion
20. grace + ous

1. **suggestion**
2. **financial**
3. **especially**
4. **digestion**
5. **commercial**
6. **exhaustion**
7. **cautious**
8. **fraction**
9. **mention**
10. **artificial**
11. **question**
12. **position**
13. **population**
14. **national**
15. **dictionary**
16. **glacier**
17. **social**
18. **precious**
19. **motion**
20. **gracious**

54

153

Name _____

Challenge Words

proceeding	preceding	envelop
envelope	emigrate	immigrate

■ Write a Challenge Word to match each definition.

1. to wrap or cover ___envelop___
2. leave one's country to settle in another ___emigrate___
3. going on after having stopped ___proceeding___
4. paper cover for mailing ___envelope___
5. coming before ___preceding___
6. come into a country to live ___immigrate___

■ Talk to family members and friends to find someone who came to this country from another country. Then use Challenge Words to write a paragraph about the person and his or her native land.

_____
_____
_____
_____
_____
_____
_____

55

Name _____

since	sense	choose	chose	finally
finely	except	accept	beside	besides

■ **Making Connections** Write the list word that matches each clue.

1. How you might chop onions for a recipe — ___finely___
2. The opposite of *reject* — ___accept___
3. What you do when you have two options — ___choose___
4. Sight, smell, touch, taste, or sound — ___sense___

■ **Word Choice** Write the correct list word for each sentence.

5. Everyone ate the eggplant (except, accept) Tim. — ___except___
6. The concert was (finely, finally) over. — ___finally___
7. Sue (choose, chose) a puppy at the pound. — ___chose___
8. No one (beside, besides) Carlo knows the code. — ___besides___
9. I haven't seen him (since, sense) yesterday. — ___since___
10. Tina put in (finely, finally) chopped parsley. — ___finely___
11. Olivia sat (besides, beside) her brother. — ___beside___

STRATEGIC SPELLING: Seeing Meaning Connections
Complete each sentence with a word from the box.

Words with *accept*			
acceptance	acceptable	acceptably	unacceptable

12. Student: "I hope my paper is ___acceptable___ ."
13. Teacher: "No, this messy work is ___unacceptable___ ."
14. Student: "How can I gain your ___acceptance___ ?"
15. Teacher: "Turn in an ___acceptably___ written paper."

56

Name _____

Word List

since	sense	choose	chose	finally
finely	except	accept	beside	besides
recent	resent	access	excess	later
latter	metal	medal	personal	personnel

■ **Word Math** Write a list word to complete each equation.

1. iron + copper + lead =
2. winner + ceremony + prize =
3. company + employee + hire =
4. private + individual + shy =
5. food + too much + stomachache =
6. ramp + wheelchair + openness =
7. insult + response + anger =
8. yesterday + new + fresh =

■ **Which Is It?** Use a list word to complete each sentence below.

9. Didn't you ___ a sweater already?
10. Yes, I ___ this wool sweater.
11. I've finished all my assignments ___ for geography.
12. Maybe Mr. Singh will ___ your homework late.
13. Lin has not practiced her flute ___ Wednesday.
14. That's strange, she usually has better ___ than that.
15. Of the two movies I saw, I preferred the ___.
16. I hope I'll get a chance to see it ___.
17. Do you want to sit ___ me at the awards dinner?
18. Yes, and how many people are coming ___ us?
19. The tomatoes have to be chopped more ___ than that.
20. Yes, I think I've ___ learned how to do it!

1. ___metal___
2. ___medal___
3. ___personnel___
4. ___personal___
5. ___excess___
6. ___access___
7. ___resent___
8. ___recent___
9. ___choose___
10. ___chose___
11. ___except___
12. ___accept___
13. ___since___
14. ___sense___
15. ___latter___
16. ___later___
17. ___beside___
18. ___besides___
19. ___finely___
20. ___finally___

57

Name _____

Word List

since	sense	choose	chose	finally
finely	except	accept	beside	besides
recent	resent	access	excess	later
latter	metal	medal	personal	personnel

■ **Synonyms** Write the list word that means the same as the words in each group below.

1. private, individual, ___
2. feeling, awareness, ___
3. approve of, agree to, ___
4. next to, near, ___
5. pick, select, ___
6. current, new, ___
7. overflow, extra, ___
8. award, prize, ___
9. at last, eventually, ___
10. staff, employees, ___

■ **Definitions** Write the list words that mean the same as the underlined words.

11. The class will begin <u>after the usual time</u>.
12. The game will stop until another time <u>because it is raining</u>.
13. John likes all candy flavors <u>but</u> licorice.
14. <u>Other than</u> these, I think I've read all the books.
15. Lee will <u>take offense</u> at any interference.
16. Randy <u>picked</u> the black shoes.
17. The <u>opening</u> to the cave was on the north side of the mountain.

■ **Seeing Relationships** Write a list word that fits the clues below.

18. This describes the second of two things.
19. This is shiny and cold.
20. Very small pieces have been chopped this way.

1. ___personal___
2. ___sense___
3. ___accept___
4. ___beside___
5. ___choose___
6. ___recent___
7. ___excess___
8. ___medal___
9. ___finally___
10. ___personnel___
11. ___later___
12. ___since___
13. ___except___
14. ___Besides___
15. ___resent___
16. ___chose___
17. ___access___
18. ___latter___
19. ___metal___
20. ___finely___

58

CHALLENGE ■ 15

Challenge Words				
exquisite	mischievous	refrigerator	pastime	anxious

■ Use Challenge Words to fill in the blanks in the following conversation.

"That crystal vase is **exquisite** ! I am so **anxious** that it might fall and break!"

"I'll put it out of reach on the **refrigerator** ."

"I'm sure my **mischievous** cat will jump up there and knock the vase down!"

"Calm down! I think worrying is your favorite **pastime** ."

■ Sometimes people create conversations to practice what to say at a party or on a job interview. Use one or more Challenge Words to write a practice interview for a job.

_____
_____
_____
_____
_____
_____
_____

59

---

15 ■ THINK AND PRACTICE

similar	doesn't	experience	forward	exactly
partner	drawer	expensive	develop	familiar

■ **Drawing Conclusions** Write the list word that answers each question.

1. Where might you keep your socks? — **drawer**
2. What can help you get a job? — **experience**
3. Who works with you? — **partner**
4. What do you do to a roll of film to get pictures? — **develop**
5. How should you do measurements? — **exactly**
6. What word would you use to describe synonyms? — **similar**

■ **Antonyms** Write the list word that completes each phrase.

7. not cheap, but **expensive**
8. not strange, but **familiar**
9. not backward, but **forward**
10. not different, but **similar**
11. not does, but **doesn't**

STRATEGIC SPELLING: Using the Memory Tricks Strategy
Use memory tricks to help you spell. Create memory tricks using the list words and helpers below. Underline the matching letters.

12. exactly—act   **Answers will vary.**

13. drawer—draw   **Answers will vary.**

14. doesn't—doe   **Answers will vary.**

15. forward—for   **Answers will vary.**

60

EXTRA PRACTICE ■ 15

Word List				
similar	doesn't	experience	forward	exactly
partner	drawer	expensive	develop	familiar
pigeon	tickling	penalty	frustrated	athletic
celebration	circling	helicopter	trembling	sparkling

■ **Classifying** Write the list word that belongs in each group below.

1. costly, high priced, ___ — 1. **expensive**
2. backward, sideways, ___ — 2. **forward**
3. dove, crow, ___ — 3. **pigeon**
4. plane, blimp, ___ — 4. **helicopter**
5. co-worker, helper, ___ — 5. **partner**
6. vigorous, acrobatic, ___ — 6. **athletic**
7. shaking, shuddering, ___ — 7. **trembling**
8. party, reception, ___ — 8. **celebration**
9. fine, punishment, ___ — 9. **penalty**
10. don't, won't, ___ — 10. **doesn't**
11. angry, dissatisfied, ___ — 11. **frustrated**

■ **Puzzle** Complete each list word in the blanks below. The circled letters will give you the answer to the riddle.

12. e x a (c) t l y
13. s i m i l a r
14. d r a w e (r)
15. e x p e r i e n (c) e
16. d e v e (l) o p
17. f a m (i) l i a r
18. t i c k l (i) n g
19. s p a r k l i n (g)

What does the captain say your plane is doing if the airport is crowded?

20. c i r c l i n g

61

---

15 ■ REVIEW

Word List				
similar	doesn't	experience	forward	exactly
partner	drawer	expensive	develop	familiar
pigeon	tickling	penalty	frustrated	athletic
celebration	circling	helicopter	trembling	sparkling

■ **Drawing Conclusions** Write the list word that answers each question.

1. What vehicle has a pinwheel top? — 1. **helicopter**
2. What's funny that you want to stop immediately? — 2. **tickling**
3. What coos and carries a message? — 3. **pigeon**
4. Who do police officers turn to for help? — 4. **partner**
5. How do white teeth look? — 5. **sparkling**
6. What does an offensive foul require? — 6. **penalty**
7. What often requires a special cake? — 7. **celebration**
8. What keeps your socks out of sight? — 8. **drawer**
9. What kind of contest is just between sports? — 9. **athletic**
10. What do employers often look for? — 10. **experience**

■ **Combining Syllables** Combine each syllable in the first column with a syllable or syllables from the second column to make a list word.

11. cir	act ly	11. **circling**
12. for	vel op	12. **forward**
13. ex	ward	13. **exactly**
14. de	trat ed	14. **develop**
15. fa	i lar	15. **familiar**
16. frus	mil iar	16. **frustrated**
17. sim	cling	17. **similar**

■ **Seeing Meaning Connections**
Complete the poem with the words below.

expensive   trembling   doesn't

It (18) take an expert,
To say with voice a' (19) ,
That beautiful jewels are (20) ,
And payments, never-ending.

18. **doesn't**
19. **trembling**
20. **expensive**

62

155

CHALLENGE ■ 16

Challenge Words		
mosquitoes	desperadoes	flamingos
wharves	bailiffs	

■ Answer the following questions using Challenge Words.

1. Which would you see in an Old West movie? **desperadoes**
2. Which insects would you find in hot, steamy weather? **mosquitoes**
3. Which would you hope to see when pleasure boating in Florida?
   flamingos
4. Which would you hope to see when docking a boat? **wharves**
5. Which work in a courtroom? **bailiffs**

■ Folktales and lore about the Old West are an important part of our culture. Write a paragraph describing your favorite story about the Old West—or make up an outline for a story of your own.

_____
_____
_____
_____
_____
_____
_____
_____

16 ■ THINK AND PRACTICE

scarfs	staffs	shelves	wolves	ourselves
solos	stereos	volcanoes	quizzes	pants

■ **Classifying** Write the list word that belongs in each group.

1. televisions, radios, **stereos**
2. quartets, duets, **solos**
3. closets, drawers, **shelves**
4. homework, exams, **quizzes**

■ **Context** Write the list word that completes each sentence.

5. Alicia wears colorful **scarfs** that match her clothes.
6. In the mountains, you can hear **wolves** howling at night.
7. We laughed at **ourselves** for forgetting the tickets.
8. The library and teaching **staffs** had a party.
9. Ivan learned how to iron a pair of **pants**
10. Mauna Loa is one of Hawaii's most famous **volcanoes** .
11. Mr. Alvarez's **shelves** are filled with books on every subject.

STRATEGIC SPELLING: Building New Words
Add either -s or -es to each word. If you're not sure how to spell the plural, look in your Spelling Dictionary.

12. belief **beliefs**
13. elf **elves**
14. echo **echoes**
15. piano **pianos**

EXTRA PRACTICE ■ 16

Word List				
scarfs	staffs	shelves	wolves	ourselves
solos	stereos	volcanoes	quizzes	pants
sheriffs	reefs	chiefs	knives	thieves
studios	dominoes	buffaloes	scissors	measles

■ **Double Plurals** Write list words to complete the sentences.

1. Dad painted the cupboards and **shelves** in the kitchen.
2. The musical program contained several duets and **solos** .
3. Sara likes to wear bright hats and **scarfs** .
4. It took several deputies and **sheriffs** to catch the outlaws.
5. Many shipwrecks have been caused by dangerous **reefs**
6. Grandma had mumps and **measles** as a child.
7. The land was devastated by earthquakes and **volcanoes**
8. This book describes how dogs and **wolves** are different.
9. Jay took all his shirts and **pants** to the cleaners.
10. They have a sale on cassette players and **stereos** .
11. Horses and **buffaloes** were important to the Plains Indians.
12. Crayons and **scissors** are supplies that you use in school.

■ **Plurals** Write the list word that is the plural form of each word below.

13. studio **studios**
14. chief **chiefs**
15. knife **knives**
16. staff **staffs**
17. thief **thieves**
18. domino **dominoes**
19. ourself **ourselves**
20. quiz **quizzes**

16 ■ REVIEW

Word List				
scarfs	staffs	shelves	wolves	ourselves
solos	stereos	volcanoes	quizzes	pants
sheriffs	reefs	chiefs	knives	thieves
studios	dominoes	buffaloes	scissors	measles

■ **Context Clues** Add -s or -es to each word in parentheses to form a list word that completes each sentence.

1. Today, (buffalo) are raised on farms.
2. We could hear the (wolf) howling nearby.
3. Let's scuba-dive off the coral (reef).
4. The (thief) broke in through the door.
5. The art (studio) will be near the river.
6. Put the (knife) on the table.
7. The (staff) of workers are being added to.
8. In the Old West, the (sheriff) once reigned.
9. The (stereo) will go on sale Friday.
10. The (volcano) erupted with great force.
11. The concert will end after the final (solo).

■ **Rhymes** Write the list word that makes sense in the verse.

12. To the midwinter dance,
    Wear your wool ___ .
13. Help yourselves
    To the pies on the ___ .
14. Scholarly whizzes
    Ace all their ___ .
15. Go to your easels
    And draw dots like ___ .
16. We don't need elves.
    We'll do it ___ .
17. A block pattern grows
    As you play ___ .

■ **Synonyms** Write the list word that means the same as each word below.

18. shears   20. leaders
19. neckwear

1. **buffaloes**
2. **wolves**
3. **reefs**
4. **thieves**
5. **studios**
6. **knives**
7. **staffs**
8. **sheriffs**
9. **stereos**
10. **volcanoes**
11. **solos**
12. **pants**
13. **shelves**
14. **quizzes**
15. **measles**
16. **ourselves**
17. **dominoes**
18. **scissors**
19. **scarfs**
20. **chiefs**

CHALLENGE ■ 17

Challenge Words		
haste	hasten	heir
inherit	harmony	harmonious

■ Complete the following sentences using the correct form of the Challenge Words.

HURRY

You make **haste** .

You **hasten** to the store.

RELATIONSHIPS

You can create **harmony** .

You can spend a **harmonious** evening with friends.

FAMILY

If your parents write a will, you are an **heir** .

You can **inherit** wealth or objects.

■ Doing things faster isn't always better. Remember the saying "haste makes waste"? Write a paragraph about a time that proved that saying to be true. Use one or more Challenge Words.

_____

_____

_____

_____

_____

_____

_____

_____

_____

_____

67

---

17 ■ THINK AND PRACTICE

human	humane	clean	cleanse	nature
natural	major	majority	poem	poetic

■ **Word Relationships** Write the list word that matches each clue. Then write the list word that is related to it.

a written work in verse 1. **poem** _____ 2. **poetic** _____

greater in importance 3. **major** _____ 4. **majority** _____

not dirty 5. **clean** _____ 6. **cleanse** _____

■ **Related Pairs** To complete each sentence, write two list words that are related.

7. Be sure to **cleanse** the cut on your finger with **clean** water.

8. Every **human** being should be **humane** to animals.

9. You may not think you are **poetic** , but you can write a good **poem** .

10. Aaron felt most **natural** when he was outdoors enjoying **nature** .

11. This **poem** has the most **poetic** description of daffodils that I have ever read.

12. It is only **natural** for animals such as lions to live in **nature** .

STRATEGIC SPELLING: Seeing Meaning Connections
Write the word from the box that completes each phrase. Use a dictionary if you need help.

| humanity |
| humanitarian |
| humanize |

13. represent as human **humanize**

14. mankind **humanity**

15. a person promoting social reform **humanitarian**

68

EXTRA PRACTICE ■ 17

Word List				
human	humane	clean	cleanse	nature
natural	major	majority	poem	poetic
equal	equation	unite	unity	bomb
bombard	muscle	muscular	resign	resignation

■ **Adding Endings** Write the list word that is formed when you add each base word and ending below.

1. resign + ation
2. nature + al
3. unite + y
4. major + ity
5. equate + ion
6. muscle + ar
7. poet + ic
8. human + e

$2+2=4$
$4+4=8$
$8+8=16$

$2 \times 2 = 4$
$4 \times 4 = 16$
$8 \times 8 = 64$

1. **resignation**
2. **natural**
3. **unity**
4. **majority**
5. **equation**
6. **muscular**
7. **poetic**
8. **humane**

■ **Variety** Write each remaining list word on the line under its description. Which words have:

—the long **e** sound?

9. **equal**

10. **clean**

—the **z** sound spelled *s*?

11. **cleanse**

12. **resign**

—the long **u** sound?

13. **unite**

14. **human**

—a silent letter?

15. **muscle**

16. **bomb**

—the **er** sound?

17. **major**

18. **nature**

—the long **o** sound?

19. **poem**

—the short **o** sound?

20. **bombard**

69

---

17 ■ REVIEW

Word List				
human	humane	clean	cleanse	nature
natural	major	majority	poem	poetic
equal	equation	unite	unity	bomb
bombard	muscle	muscular	resign	resignation

■ **Classifying** Write the list word that belongs in each group.

1. bone, tendon, ___
2. spotless, immaculate, ___
3. unspoiled, unaffected, ___
4. kind, charitable, ___
5. important, large, ___
6. retirement, termination, ___
7. grenade, missile, ___
8. join, combine, ___
9. rhythmic, rhyming, ___
10. same, identical, ___

■ **Complete a Poem** Write list words to complete the poem.

The minority—no, the (11)—yes,
Answered the math (12) with a guess.
To (13) my mind of number thought,
I wrote a verse of a (14) on the spot.
It goes: A (15) being is what I am.
It's not in my (16) to like to cram.
So please slow down when things get hard,
With numbers, please do not (17).

■ **Antonyms** Write the list word that means the opposite of each word below.

18. division
19. puny
20. join

1. **muscle**
2. **clean**
3. **natural**
4. **humane**
5. **major**
6. **resignation**
7. **bomb**
8. **unite**
9. **poetic**
10. **equal**
11. **majority**
12. **equation**
13. **cleanse**
14. **poem**
15. **human**
16. **nature**
17. **bombard**
18. **unity**
19. **muscular**
20. **resign**

70

Name _____

Lesson 13

precious	commercial	dictionary	question	population

■ **Classifying** Write the list word that belongs in each group.

1. advertisement, message, __commercial__
2. encyclopedia, almanac, __dictionary__
3. people, inhabitants, __population__
4. valuable, expensive, __precious__
5. inquiry, request, __question__

Lesson 14

choose	finely	except	beside	sense

■ **Context** Write the list word that completes each sentence.

1. When you mince parsley, you chop it __finely__.
2. Remember to use common __sense__ in an emergency.
3. We stood quietly __beside__ the crib.
4. Which sweater did you __choose__?
5. Everyone __except__ Matt went to the game.

Lesson 15

similar	experience	exactly	partner	familiar

■ **Definitions** Write the list word that means the same as the underlined word or words.

1. My person who shares and I drew a map. __partner__
2. Do you have any practice working with pets? __experience__
3. That music sounds well-known to me. __familiar__
4. The book costs precisely seven dollars. __exactly__
5. This building looks very much the same to that one. __similar__

Name _____

Lesson 16

wolves	volcanoes	staffs	solos	pants

■ **Word Forms** Write the list word that is the plural form of each word.

1. volcano __volcanoes__
2. pants __pants__
3. solo __solos__
4. wolf __wolves__
5. staff __staffs__

Lesson 17

humane	clean	nature	majority	poetic

■ **Seeing Relationships** Write the list word that matches each clue.

1. If you write a poem, then you are this. __poetic__
2. If something is all natural, then it comes from this. __nature__
3. A human who is kind to animals is said to be this. __humane__
4. If you cleanse something, then it will be this. __clean__
5. To make a major change, sometimes this is needed. __majority__

CHALLENGE ■ 19

Challenge Words				
pessimism	prominent	controversy	suspicious	porpoise

■ Use Challenge Words to complete the relationships described below.

Pessimism _____ is to optimism as bad news is to good news.

Suspicious _____ is to trusting as approval is to disapproval.

Porpoise _____ is to whale as chimpanzee is to ape.

Controversy _____ is to consensus as disagreement is to agreement.

Prominent _____ is to noticeable as new is to unused.

■ Zoos are the setting for exciting programs to save, breed, and restore the health of animals. Use one or more Challenge Words to write a paragraph of zoo news.

_____
_____
_____
_____
_____
_____
_____
_____
_____
_____
_____
_____
_____
_____

Everyday Spelling © Scott Foresman • Addison Wesley

73

---

19 ■ THINK AND PRACTICE

different	register	carnival	variety	atmosphere
favorite	pattern	understand	sentence	instance

■ **Synonyms** Write a list word that means the same as the underlined word.

1. Mario won a prize at the <u>fair</u>.   **carnival**
2. Tara did not <u>comprehend</u> the question.   **understand**
3. The wallpaper had a flowered <u>design</u>.   **pattern**
4. Macaroni is Keesha's <u>preferred</u> food.   **favorite**
5. The salad had an interesting <u>mixture</u> of fruits.   **variety**

■ **Definitions** Write the list word that fits each definition.

6. a group of words that states a complete thought   **sentence**
7. not the same as   **different**
8. an example or illustration   **instance**
9. one that is liked best   **favorite**
10. the air surrounding the earth   **atmosphere**
11. to enroll or sign up   **register**

STRATEGIC SPELLING: Using the Divide and Conquer Strategy
Sometimes it helps to study long words piece by piece. Write four list words that are hard for you. Draw lines between the syllables. Then study the words syllable by syllable. Check the Spelling Dictionary if you need help.

12. **Answers will vary.**   14. **Answers will vary.**

13. **Answers will vary.**   15. **Answers will vary.**

Everyday Spelling © Scott Foresman • Addison Wesley

74

EXTRA PRACTICE ■ 19

Word List				
different	register	carnival	variety	atmosphere
favorite	pattern	understand	sentence	instance
elegant	aquarium	communicate	gasoline	factory
definite	Chicago	heavily	garage	illustrate

■ **Pronunciations** Write a list word for each pronunciation.

1. (fak′tər ē)
2. (fā′vər it)
3. (def′ə nit)
4. (dif′ər ənt)
5. (gə razh′)
6. (gas′ə lēn′)
7. (shə kô′gō)
8. (kär′nə vəl)
9. (il′ə strāt)
10. (in′stəns)
11. (hev′ə lē)
12. (və rī′ə tē)

1. **factory**
2. **favorite**
3. **definite**
4. **different**
5. **garage**
6. **gasoline**
7. **Chicago**
8. **carnival**
9. **illustrate**
10. **instance**
11. **heavily**
12. **variety**

■ **Base Words** Write the list word that is the base word for each word below.

13. sentences
14. unregistered
15. misunderstanding
16. elegantly
17. communicable
18. aquariums
19. atmospheric
20. patterning

13. **sentence**
14. **register**
15. **understand**
16. **elegant**
17. **communicate**
18. **aquarium**
19. **atmosphere**
20. **pattern**

Everyday Spelling © Scott Foresman • Addison Wesley

75

---

19 ■ REVIEW

Word List				
different	register	carnival	variety	atmosphere
favorite	pattern	understand	sentence	instance
elegant	aquarium	communicate	gasoline	factory
definite	Chicago	heavily	garage	illustrate

■ **Word Math** Answer each problem with a list word.

1. machines + manufacture = ___
2. cotton candy + rides + people = ___
3. station + tank + hose = ___
4. fish + water + tank = ___
5. noun + verb + period = ___
6. cars + tools + service people = ___
7. air + moisture + heat = ___

1. **factory**
2. **carnival**
3. **gasoline**
4. **aquarium**
5. **sentence**
6. **garage**
7. **atmosphere**

■ **Analogies** Write the list word that completes each analogy.

8. Skip is to lightly as plod is to ___.
9. St. Louis is to Missouri as ___ is to Illinois.
10. Insecure is to doubtful as assured is to ___.
11. Attend is to enroll as vote is to ___.
12. Pencil is to write as brush is to ___.
13. Limousine is to luxurious as gown is to ___.
14. Drawing is to outline as sew is to ___.
15. Liver is to dreaded as chocolate is to ___.

8. **heavily**
9. **Chicago**
10. **definite**
11. **register**
12. **illustrate**
13. **elegant**
14. **pattern**
15. **favorite**

■ **Context Clues** Write the list word that completes each sentence.

16. Do you ___ fractions?
17. There wasn't a single ___ of tardiness the whole week.
18. Try to ___ your differences calmly.
19. There's a ___ of fruits to pick from.
20. Take a ___ approach if this one doesn't work.

16. **understand**
17. **instance**
18. **communicate**
19. **variety**
20. **different**

Everyday Spelling © Scott Foresman • Addison Wesley

76

159

CHALLENGE ■ 20

Challenge Words				
enlighten	toboggan	pummel	disentangle	denominator

■ Use Challenge Words to solve the clues below. Then use the combined clues to spell vertically the word meaning "lower part of a fraction."

1. beat with fists
2. instruct
3. sort out
4. long, narrow sled

```
              d
  p u m m e l  e
              n
              o
              m
  ²e n l i g h t e n
              n
  ³d i s e n t a n g l e
              t
      ⁴t o b o g g a n
              r
```

■ Skating, sledding, and tobogganing are winter sports. Choose a sport and write a paragraph that persuades a friend to participate in your sport. Use one or more Challenge Words.

_____
_____
_____
_____
_____
_____
_____

77

20 ■ THINK AND PRACTICE

slogan	citizen	forgotten	propeller	collector
level	tunnel	double	single	example

■ **Associations** Write the list word that is related to each item.

1. one — **single**
2. instance — **example**
3. advertising — **slogan**
4. taxpayer — **citizen**
5. helicopter — **propeller**
6. forgiven — **forgotten**

■ **Analogies** Write the list word that completes each analogy.

7. Three is to triple as two is to **double** .
8. Over is to bridge as through is to **tunnel** .
9. Crooked is to uneven as smooth is to **level** .
10. Perform is to performer as collect is to **collector** .
11. Loved is to hated as remembered is to **forgotten** .

STRATEGIC SPELLING: Seeing Meaning Connections
Write the words from the box that fit the definitions.

Words related to *collect*	
collector	collection
collectible	recollect

12. to remember — **recollect**
13. an object that is gathered in a group as a hobby — **collectible**
14. one who accumulates objects for study or as a hobby — **collector**
15. a group of objects — **collection**

78

EXTRA PRACTICE ■ 20

Word List				
slogan	citizen	forgotten	propeller	collector
level	tunnel	double	single	example
urban	orphan	kindergarten	encounter	conquer
appetizer	dishonor	tractor	easel	recycle

■ **Analogies** Use a list word to complete each sentence below.

1. Teenager is to high school as child is to ___.
2. Garage is to car as barn is to ___.
3. Water is to pipe as cars are to ___.
4. Club is to member as nation is to ___.
5. Observe is to examine as defeat is to ___.
6. Farm is to rural as factory is to ___.
7. Mountain is to uneven as plateau is to ___.
8. Inspect is to inspector as collect is to ___.
9. Writer is to notebook as painter is to ___.
10. Inform is to news story as persuade is to ___.

■ **Making Inferences** Write a list word to match each clue.

11. This gets you to first base.
12. A puppy without a mother or father is this.
13. This is something like a model.
14. We do this to ourselves when we betray a friend.
15. This is a fancy word for a meeting.
16. You might have done this when you weren't reminded.
17. This gets you to second base.
18. Too much of this spoils your dinner.
19. This is not needed by a jet plane.
20. Do this to help conserve the earth's resources.

1. **kindergarten**
2. **tractor**
3. **tunnel**
4. **citizen**
5. **conquer**
6. **urban**
7. **level**
8. **collector**
9. **easel**
10. **slogan**
11. **single**
12. **orphan**
13. **example**
14. **dishonor**
15. **encounter**
16. **forgotten**
17. **double**
18. **appetizer**
19. **propeller**
20. **recycle**

79

20 ■ REVIEW

Word List				
slogan	citizen	forgotten	propeller	collector
level	tunnel	double	single	example
urban	orphan	kindergarten	encounter	conquer
appetizer	dishonor	tractor	easel	recycle

■ **Complete a Poem** Complete the poem with list words.

I liked drawing on the _(1)_.
When I was five in _(2)_.
I did it every _(3)_ day.
I have remembered, not _(4)_.
Now I _(5)_ through the dirt
To _(6)_ foes down deep.
For I'm an avid rock _(7)_.
The best of rocks I keep.

■ **Context Clues** Write the list word that completes each sentence.

8. The ___ for the ad is funny.
9. The ___ on the chalkboard helped the class do the problem.
10. We're helping to ___ waste materials.
11. The farmer climbed onto the ___.
12. A ___ has many rights, but also many responsibilities.
13. The airplane's ___ broke loose from the motor.
14. The twins' criminal life brought ___ to their family.
15. Many rivers around ___ areas are polluted.
16. The ___ was adopted immediately.

■ **Classifying** Write the list word that belongs in each group.

17. twice, twofold, ___
18. soup, salad, ___
19. even, straight, ___
20. meet, confront, ___

1. **easel**
2. **kindergarten**
3. **single**
4. **forgotten**
5. **tunnel**
6. **conquer**
7. **collector**
8. **slogan**
9. **example**
10. **recycle**
11. **tractor**
12. **citizen**
13. **propeller**
14. **dishonor**
15. **urban**
16. **orphan**
17. **double**
18. **appetizer**
19. **level**
20. **encounter**

80

Everyday Spelling © Scott Foresman • Addison Wesley

CHALLENGE ■ 21

Challenge Words				
informative	remorseful	trustworthy	furthermore	observable

■ Find the Challenge Word that fits the clue. Then write a sentence using that word.

1. full of facts **informative: Children's sentences will vary.**
2. in addition **furthermore: Children's sentences will vary.**
3. visible **observable: Children's sentences will vary.**
4. reliable **trustworthy: Children's sentences will vary.**
5. sorry for **remorseful: Children's sentences will vary.**

■ Imagine that someone is on trial for a crime he or she did not commit. You are the lawyer for the defense. Use one or more Challenge Words to introduce your client to the jury.

_____
_____
_____
_____
_____
_____
_____
_____
_____
_____

21 ■ THINK AND PRACTICE

report	order	explore	ignore	expert
service	research	worth	worst	disturb

■ **Base Words** Write the list word that is the base word of each word.

1. serviceable **service**
2. inexpert **expert**
3. disturbance **disturb**
4. exploratory **explore**
5. disorder **order**

■ **Context** Write the list word that is missing from each person's statement.

6. Scientist: "I have done **research** on earthquakes."
7. Jeweler: "Your diamond ring is **worth** thousands of dollars."
8. Dentist: "Don't **ignore** a pain in your tooth."
9. Newscaster: "Stay tuned for a special **report**."
10. Meteorologist: "This is the **worst** flooding in thirty years."

STRATEGIC SPELLING: Building New Words
Complete the chart by adding **-ed** and **-ing** to each of these words: report, ignore, order, research, explore.

Add -ed	Add -ing
11. **reported**	**reporting**
12. **ignored**	**ignoring**
13. **ordered**	**ordering**
14. **researched**	**researching**
15. **explored**	**exploring**

EXTRA PRACTICE ■ 21

Word List				
report	order	explore	ignore	expert
service	research	worth	worst	disturb
sword	forty	enormous	therefore	determine
permanent	earning	thorough	attorney	purchase

■ **Making Inferences** Write the list word that each sentence makes you think of.

1. Juan has two twenty-dollar bills.
2. That was the most awful TV show I've ever seen.
3. Are they going to sue the company?
4. Ahmed knows more about the solar system than anyone.
5. Are you going to buy a new car this year?
6. This medieval weapon is still in good condition.
7. The structure has been made to last a long time.
8. Why do you always interrupt me when I'm practicing?
9. Kim plans to study rain forest plants and animals.
10. The monster in the film filled the screen.

1. **forty**
2. **worst**
3. **attorney**
4. **expert**
5. **purchase**
6. **sword**
7. **permanent**
8. **disturb**
9. **research**
10. **enormous**

■ **How Is It Spelled?** Write each remaining list word in the column that tells how it is spelled.

ér sound spelled er
11. **service**
12. **determine**

ér sound spelled or
13. **worth**
14. **thorough**

ér sound spelled ear
15. **earning**

ôr sound spelled or
16. **order**
17. **report**

ôr sound spelled ore
18. **ignore**
19. **therefore**
20. **explore**

21 ■ REVIEW

Word List				
report	order	explore	ignore	expert
service	research	worth	worst	disturb
sword	forty	enormous	therefore	determine
permanent	earning	thorough	attorney	purchase

■ **Antonyms** Write the list word that completes each phrase.

1. not the *best*, but the __
2. not *see to*, but __
3. not *temporary*, but __
4. not *sell*, but __
5. not *amateur*, but __
6. not *tiny*, but __
7. not *spending*, but __
8. not *partial*, but __

■ **Classifying** Write the list word that belongs in each group.

9. judge, bailiff, __
10. four, fourteen, __
11. demand, command, __
12. talk, presentation, __
13. bother, trouble, __
14. seek, quest, __
15. so, after all, __
16. decide, conclude, __
17. lance, helmet, __

■ **Synonyms in Context** Write a list word that means about the same as the underlined word or words in each sentence.

18. He did me the <u>favor</u> of raking the leaves.
19. The antiques' <u>value</u> is unknown.
20. Look up magazine articles as part of your <u>investigation</u>.

1. **worst**
2. **ignore**
3. **permanent**
4. **purchase**
5. **expert**
6. **enormous**
7. **earning**
8. **thorough**
9. **attorney**
10. **forty**
11. **order**
12. **report**
13. **disturb**
14. **explore**
15. **therefore**
16. **determine**
17. **sword**
18. **service**
19. **worth**
20. **research**

CHALLENGE ■ 22

Challenge Words

administration   investigation   exhibition   prescription   cancellation

■ Write the Challenge Word by adding the suffix.

1. administer **administration**
2. investigate **investigation**
3. exhibit **exhibition**
4. prescribe **prescription**
5. cancel **cancellation**

■ Imagine you are an art critic attending a big exhibition. Use one or more Challenge Words to write your review about the art gallery.

_____

_____

_____

_____

_____

_____

_____

---

22 ■ THINK AND PRACTICE

| relaxation | exploration | occupation | destination | infection |
| collection | reaction | situation | television | convention |

■ **Making Connections** Write the list word that tells what each person has.

1. collector **collection**
2. video viewer **television**
3. employee **occupation**
4. traveler **destination**
5. patient **infection**

■ **Context Clues** Add a suffix to each word in parentheses to form a list word to complete each sentence.

6. The beach is a good place for (relax). **relaxation**
7. What was Tricia's (react) to the surprise party? **reaction**
8. They have a (convene) every four years. **convention**
9. Marine biologists perform underwater (explore). **exploration**
10. Joe was in the hospital with a serious (infect). **infection**
11. How would you handle the (situate)? **situation**

STRATEGIC SPELLING: Building New Words
Add the suffix -tion to the following base words:
deceive, reduce, resolve, assume. Use your Spelling Dictionary if you need help.

12. **deception**   14. **resolution**
13. **reduction**   15. **assumption**

EXTRA PRACTICE ■ 22

Word List

relaxation	exploration	occupation	destination	infection
collection	reaction	situation	television	convention
orientation	recommendation	determination	generation	reflection
destruction	attention	deduction	reception	solution

■ **Words in Context** Write a list word to complete each person's statement below.

1. Mother: "The people in your grandfather's ___ lived through the Depression."
2. Math Teacher: "What ___ did you get to that problem?"
3. Museum Guide: "This is a fine ___ of Egyptian art."
4. Clerk: "With a price ___ of 10%, your charge will be $7.56."
5. Engineer: "This new ___ set is computer controlled."
6. City Official: "The ___ caused by the storm was extensive."
7. Astronomer: "The ___ of the solar system has told much about Earth."
8. Police Officer: "A ___ is never hopeless."
9. Doctor: "Use this cream to avoid ___."
10. Announcer: "May I have your ___, please!"
11. Counselor: "We will have middle school ___ all week."
12. Job Interviewer: "What was your last ___?"

■ **Riddles** Write the list word that matches each clue.

13. a warm bath
14. a full meeting hall
15. someone jumping in fright
16. gritted teeth
17. a lake with a smooth surface
18. a road map
19. the picture on a TV set
20. a letter full of praise

1. **generation**
2. **solution**
3. **collection**
4. **deduction**
5. **television**
6. **destruction**
7. **exploration**
8. **situation**
9. **infection**
10. **attention**
11. **orientation**
12. **occupation**
13. **relaxation**
14. **convention**
15. **reaction**
16. **determination**
17. **reflection**
18. **destination**
19. **reception**
20. **recommendation**

---

22 ■ REVIEW

Word List

relaxation	exploration	occupation	destination	infection
collection	reaction	situation	television	convention
orientation	recommendation	determination	generation	reflection
destruction	attention	deduction	reception	solution

■ **Associations** Write the list word that is associated with each item below.

1. channel selector
2. equation
3. mirror
4. outer space
5. static
6. bacteria
7. vacation
8. baseball cards
9. nuclear explosion
10. Sherlock Holmes
11. political party

■ **Word Forms** Write the list word that contains the base word below.

12. recommend
13. orient
14. react

■ **Synonyms** Write the list word that means the same as the words in each group below.

15. state, predicament, ___
16. job, career, ___
17. resolve, purpose, ___
18. mother, grandmother, ___
19. goal, target, ___
20. interest, concentration, ___

1. **television**
2. **solution**
3. **reflection**
4. **exploration**
5. **reception**
6. **infection**
7. **relaxation**
8. **collection**
9. **destruction**
10. **deduction**
11. **convention**
12. **recommendation**
13. **orientation**
14. **reaction**
15. **situation**
16. **occupation**
17. **determination**
18. **generation**
19. **destination**
20. **attention**

CHALLENGE ■ 23

Challenge Words				
succotash	artichoke	sauerkraut	won ton	chutney

■ Use Challenge Words and the list of clues to complete the puzzle below. Then read the word in the dark box that tells about all these foods.

```
        w o n t o n
²s u c c o t a s h
        ³s a u e r k r a u t
        ⁴a r t i c h o k e
⁵t h u t n e y
```

Foods of the World
1. Chinese
2. Native American
3. German
4. Italian
5. Indian

■ New foods can add zest to the dinner table and spice to life. Use one or more Challenge Words to describe a special feast, a new food, or food festival you have enjoyed.

_____
_____
_____
_____
_____
_____
_____
_____
_____

89

---

23 ■ THINK AND PRACTICE

moose	cobra	alligator	vanilla	banana
tomato	mustard	hula	picnic	barbecue

■ **Complete a Poem** Write list words to complete the poem.

Yellow _(1)_ on a hot dog bun, 1. **mustard**

An old _(2)_ table in the sun. 2. **picnic**

A ripe red _(3)_ tastes supreme, 3. **tomato**

Followed by cool _(4)_ ice cream. 4. **vanilla**

Part of the fun of a _(5)_ 5. **barbecue**

Is what you taste and what you view!

■ **Classifying** Write the list word that belongs in each group.

6. waltz, jig, **hula**

7. apple, pear, **banana**

8. crocodile, lizard, **alligator**

9. copperhead, rattlesnake, **cobra**

10. reindeer, elk, **moose**

11. chocolate, strawberry, **vanilla**

STRATEGIC SPELLING: Using the Divide and Conquer Strategy
Write four list words that are hard for you. Draw lines between the syllables. Check the Spelling Dictionary if you need help. Then study the words syllable by syllable.

12. **Answers will vary.** 14. **Answers will vary.**

13. **Answers will vary.** 15. **Answers will vary.**

90

EXTRA PRACTICE ■ 23

Word List				
moose	cobra	alligator	vanilla	banana
tomato	mustard	hula	picnic	barbecue
crocodile	coyote	koala	macaroni	catsup
polka	ballet	waltz	banquet	buffet

■ **Analogies** Use a list word to complete each analogy below.

1. Bark is to dog as howl is to __.
2. Green is to relish as red is to __.
3. Oven is to bake as grill is to __.
4. Suffocate is to boa constrictor as poison is to __.
5. Informal is to picnic as formal is to __.
6. Rind is to orange as skin is to __.
7. Folk dance is to square dance as ballroom dance is to __.
8. United States is to eagle as Australia is to __.
9. Dairy product is to milk as flavoring is to __.
10. Mexico is to hat dance as Hawaii is to __.

■ **Making Inferences** Write a list word to match each clue below.

11. You need to stand on tiptoe to do this.
12. This is a seedy sort of food.
13. You'll share this with ants.
14. This will spice up your meal.
15. Have all you can eat, but serve yourself.
16. This creature has a lot of headgear.
17. If you can hop to it, you'll do fine.
18. This goes best with cheese.
19. See you later, __.
20. In a while, __.

1. **coyote**
2. **catsup**
3. **barbecue**
4. **cobra**
5. **banquet**
6. **banana**
7. **waltz**
8. **koala**
9. **vanilla**
10. **hula**
11. **ballet**
12. **tomato**
13. **picnic**
14. **mustard**
15. **buffet**
16. **moose**
17. **polka**
18. **macaroni**
19. **alligator**
20. **crocodile**

91

---

23 ■ REVIEW

Word List				
moose	cobra	alligator	vanilla	banana
tomato	mustard	hula	picnic	barbecue
crocodile	coyote	koala	macaroni	catsup
polka	ballet	waltz	banquet	buffet

■ **Analogies** Write the list word that completes each analogy.

1. Crisp is to apple as juicy is to __.
2. Chicken is to fry as steak is to __.
3. Platter is to dinner as basket is to __.
4. Cobbler is to peach as cream pie is to __.
5. Bear is to grizzly as snake is to __.
6. Food is to flavoring as yogurt is to __.
7. Guitar is to jitterbug as accordion is to __.
8. Horn is to buffalo as antler is to __.
9. Corsage is to prom as lei is to __.
10. Apple is to applesauce as tomato is to __.

■ **Definitions** Write the list word that answers each question.

11. What word is a big meal that is served?
12. What word is a prairie wolf?
13. What word is a yellow sauce?
14. What word is an old-fashioned, slow dance?
15. What reptile looks like an alligator?
16. What word is a furry Australian?
17. What word toe-dances?
18. What word often comes with a long, strong table?
19. What word is tubes of pasta?
20. What reptile is similar to a crocodile?

1. **tomato**
2. **barbecue**
3. **picnic**
4. **banana**
5. **cobra**
6. **vanilla**
7. **polka**
8. **moose**
9. **hula**
10. **catsup**
11. **banquet**
12. **coyote**
13. **mustard**
14. **waltz**
15. **crocodile**
16. **koala**
17. **ballet**
18. **buffet**
19. **macaroni**
20. **alligator**

92

Name _____

Lesson 19

different	variety	favorite	sentence	instance

■ **Alpha Order** Write the list word that fits alphabetically in each group.

1. senior **sentence** separate
2. fault **favorite** fawn
3. diesel **different** difficult
4. inspect **instance** instrument
5. vapor **variety** vary

Lesson 20

tunnel	propeller	collector	single	slogan

■ **Riddles** Write the list word that answers each riddle.

1. I end with **er** and am found on a helicopter. **propeller**
2. I end with **an** and am a saying. **slogan**
3. I end with **le** and mean "one." **single**
4. I end with **el** and go through a mountain. **tunnel**
5. I end with **or** and like to save things. **collector**

Lesson 21

worth	disturb	expert	report	ignore

■ **Classifying** Write the list word that has the same spelling and vowel sound as the words in each group.

1. service, nerve, **expert**
2. thorn, foreign, **report**
3. nurse, turn, **disturb**
4. explore, deplore, **ignore**
5. attorney, thorough, **worth**

93

Name _____

24B ■ REVIEW

Lesson 22

exploration	occupation	convention	collection	television

■ **Word Forms** Add **-ation, -tion,** or **-ion** to each word to create a list word.

1. televise **television**
2. occupy **occupation**
3. explore **exploration**
4. convene **convention**
5. collect **collection**

Lesson 23

alligator	vanilla	tomato	mustard	picnic

■ **Drawing Conclusions** Write the list word that matches each clue.

1. Combine me with lettuce to make a salad. **tomato**
2. Squirt me on a hot dog. **mustard**
3. Choose me as an ice cream flavor. **vanilla**
4. Enjoy me as an outdoor feast. **picnic**
5. Watch out for my jaws full of sharp teeth. **alligator**

94

Everyday Spelling © Scott Foresman • Addison Wesley

Everyday Spelling © Scott Foresman • Addison Wesley

CHALLENGE ■ 25

Challenge Words

antidote   counterfeit   environmental   guarantee   sophomore

■ Write a Challenge Word for each clue.

1. **antidote** _____ : counteracts a poison
2. **sophomore** _____ : has one year fewer than a junior
3. **environmental** _____ : shows thought for the earth
4. **guarantee** _____ : can take the risk out of buying a product
5. **counterfeit** _____ : phony; not real

■ The rain forests of the world are important to our environment. Use one or more Challenge Words to write a description of a rain forest, or an account of an expedition into a rain forest.

_____
_____
_____
_____
_____
_____
_____

95

---

25 ■ THINK AND PRACTICE

| probably | cabinet | separate | wondering | clothes |
| temperature | average | beginning | restaurant | promise |

■ **Associations** Write the list word that is associated with each item.

1. maybe — **probably**
2. chef — **restaurant**
3. ending — **beginning**
4. weather — **temperature**
5. fashions — **clothes**

■ **Context Clues** Complete each sentence with a list word.

6. Linda made a **promise** _____ that she would write to me.
7. The girls were **wondering** _____ whether it would rain.
8. At the **beginning** _____ of each day, Mr. Santiago makes announcements to the students.
9. The Browns' **average** _____ grocery bill is $125 per week.
10. Each sister has a **separate** _____ bedroom.
11. The plates are in the kitchen **cabinet** _____ by the door.

STRATEGIC SPELLING: Pronouncing for Spelling
We sometimes spell words wrong because we say them wrong. Write *probably, cabinet, temperature,* and *wondering.* Now say each word slowly and carefully. Be sure to pronounce the sounds of the underlined letters.

12. **probably** _____
13. **cabinet** _____
14. **temperature** _____
15. **wondering** _____

96

EXTRA PRACTICE ■ 25

Word List

probably	cabinet	separate	wondering	clothes
temperature	average	beginning	restaurant	promise
aspirin	desperate	awfully	fishhook	twelfth
skiing	unwritten	roughly	schedule	overrule

■ **Classifying** Write the list word that belongs in each group below.

1. rod, reel, ___
2. pills, medicine, ___
3. cupboard, closet, ___
4. tenth, eleventh, ___
5. pledge, vow, ___
6. heat, measurement, ___
7. harshly, severely, ___
8. sledding, tobogganing, ___
9. outfits, garments, ___
10. diner, cafeteria, ___
11. timetable, directory, ___
12. divide, split up, ___

■ **Word Hints** Use the underlined word in each sentence to help you find the correct list word. Write each word.

13. This character would ___ never rob anyone.
14. We beg you, start at the ___.
15. I'm ___ sorry I can't eat more, but I'm too full.
16. He was so ___ he ate all the sandwiches.
17. We think you did err to ___ the vote.
18. Rae can't turn in her theme because it is ___.
19. Heather was in a rage over her ___ grade.
20. I was ___ if you would ring me today.

1. **fishhook**
2. **aspirin**
3. **cabinet**
4. **twelfth**
5. **promise**
6. **temperature**
7. **roughly**
8. **skiing**
9. **clothes**
10. **restaurant**
11. **schedule**
12. **separate**
13. **probably**
14. **beginning**
15. **awfully**
16. **desperate**
17. **overrule**
18. **unwritten**
19. **average**
20. **wondering**

97

---

25 ■ REVIEW

Word List

probably	cabinet	separate	wondering	clothes
temperature	average	beginning	restaurant	promise
aspirin	desperate	awfully	fishhook	twelfth
skiing	unwritten	roughly	schedule	overrule

■ **Synonyms** Write the list word that means the same as each word or phrase below.

1. terribly
2. likely
3. apart
4. so-so
5. starting
6. pledge
7. diner
8. wardrobe
9. cupboard
10. puzzling over
11. forlorn

■ **Word Search** Find the nine list words in the puzzle. They may be printed across or down. Write them.

```
t e m p e r a t u r e
u n w r i t t e n l n
t w e l f t h s m y g
w t d a f u t c t s r
o b v s e s n h u o i
v e s p c l k e b p q
e a h r k m c u q o m
r j g i o v b l z o n
r i a n r p h e u o l
u k n p h e u o n
l f i s h h o o k r o
e l a d t i t o d e a
b r o u g h l y m l
```

1. **awfully**
2. **probably**
3. **separate**
4. **average**
5. **beginning**
6. **promise**
7. **restaurant**
8. **clothes**
9. **cabinet**
10. **wondering**
11. **desperate**
12. **temperature**
13. **unwritten**
14. **twelfth**
15. **skiing**
16. **fishhook**
17. **roughly**
18. **overrule**
19. **aspirin**
20. **schedule**

98

CHALLENGE ■ 26

Challenge Words
comparative   apprenticeship   compassionate   alienate   appreciative

■ Use Challenge Words from the list above to complete the following sentences.

1. We did a __comparative__ study of prices before we bought this bike.
2. I feel deeply __appreciative__ for all of your help.
3. Don't __alienate__ the dog by teasing him.
4. Her __apprenticeship__ helped her learn a lot about mixing paint.
5. The doctor's __compassionate__ care helped the patient feel better.

■ Learning a new craft or skill can be a great adventure. Write a paragraph about a girl or boy who gets a chance to learn from a master. Use one or more Challenge Words in your narrative.

_____
_____
_____
_____
_____
_____
_____
_____
_____
_____
_____

99

---

26 ■ THINK AND PRACTICE

originate	fortunate	activate	attractive	inventive
negative	creative	friendship	championship	leadership

■ **Antonyms** Write the list word that means the opposite of each word.

1. positive   __negative__
2. unlucky   __fortunate__
3. unappealing   __attractive__
4. finish   __originate__

■ **Adding Suffixes** Add a suffix to each word in parentheses to form a list word that completes the sentence.

5. (champion) The soccer team won the city __championship__.
6. (leader) President Roosevelt was known for his __leadership__ during World War II.
7. (invent) A very __inventive__ student won first prize at the science fair.
8. (create) Van Gogh was a __creative__ painter.
9. (active) Do you know how to __activate__ the house's alarm system?
10. (friend) The __friendship__ between the gorilla and the kitten amazed everyone who saw it.
11. (origin) The bicycle race will __originate__ in Sioux City, Iowa, and finish in Chicago, Illinois.

STRATEGIC SPELLING: Building New Words
To make new words, add one of the suffixes to each of these base words: *partner, select, citizen, effect.*

Add -ship

12. __partnership__
13. __citizenship__

Add -ive

14. __selective__
15. __effective__

100

EXTRA PRACTICE ■ 26

Word List
originate	fortunate	activate	attractive
inventive	negative	creative	friendship
championship	leadership	affectionate	considerate
obligate	productive	defective	constructive
ownership	membership	hardship	relationship

■ **Making Inferences** Write a list word to match each clue below.

1. a new bike whose brakes don't work
2. feeling lucky
3. chronic illness
4. being part of a club
5. a clothing model
6. winning the playoff game
7. giving commands
8. cuddling a cat or dog
9. being an owner
10. shaking one's head "no"

1. __defective__
2. __fortunate__
3. __hardship__
4. __membership__
5. __attractive__
6. __championship__
7. __leadership__
8. __affectionate__
9. __ownership__
10. __negative__

■ **Puzzle** Fill in the blanks with list words. The letters in the circles will answer the riddle.

11. c o n s i d e r a t e
12. o r i g i n a t e
13. a c t i v a t e
14. f r i e n d s h i p
15. r e l a t i o n s h i p
16. p r o d u c t i v e
17. c o n s t r u c t i v e
18. c r e a t i v e
19. o b l i g a t e

What do you have to be in order to solve puzzles?

20. i n v e n t i v e

101

---

26 ■ REVIEW

Word List
originate	fortunate	activate	attractive
inventive	negative	creative	friendship
championship	leadership	affectionate	considerate
obligate	productive	defective	constructive
ownership	membership	hardship	relationship

■ **The Riddle Ship** Write the list word that answers each riddle.

1. What *ship* is for presidents?
2. What *ship* is for clubs and groups?
3. What *ship* is for Super Bowl winners?
4. What *ship* is for rocks?
5. What *ship* is for family?
6. What *ship* has a possessive atmosphere?
7. What *ship* likes all the other ships?

■ **Synonyms** Write the list word that means the same as the underlined word or phrase.

8. The new toaster is broken.
9. Remembering to call was thoughtful of you.
10. That hairdo is good-looking on you.
11. You turn on the machine by pushing that button.
12. Will the contract force us to make future purchases?
13–14. Make at least some of the criticism positive rather than unfavorable.

■ **Adding Endings** Write the list words formed by adding -ive or -ate.

15. product + ive
16. origin + ate
17. create + ive
18. fortune + ate
19. invent + ive
20. affection + ate

1. __leadership__
2. __membership__
3. __championship__
4. __hardship__
5. __relationship__
6. __ownership__
7. __friendship__
8. __defective__
9. __considerate__
10. __attractive__
11. __activate__
12. __obligate__
13. __constructive__
14. __negative__
15. __productive__
16. __originate__
17. __creative__
18. __fortunate__
19. __inventive__
20. __affectionate__

102

CHALLENGE ■ 27

Challenge Words

internally   posthumous   premonition   underachiever   overemphasize

■ Write a Challenge Word for each definition.

1. inside **internally**
2. give too much emphasis **overemphasize**
3. happening after death **posthumous**
4. works below level of ability **underachiever**
5. a forewarning **premonition**

■ Some people are quiet and shy about their accomplishments. Write a paragraph about a quiet person who has secretly done amazing things. Use one or more Challenge Words in your paragraph.

_____
_____
_____
_____
_____
_____
_____
_____
_____
_____
_____
_____
_____

---

27 ■ THINK AND PRACTICE

pretrial	prearrange	postdate	postwar	overcook
overlook	overflow	undercover	include	exclude

■ **Definitions** Write the list word that fits each definition.

1. to make preparations ahead of time **prearrange**
2. after a period of armed conflict **postwar**
3. to heat a food for too long **overcook**
4. in the time before a legal case goes to court **pretrial**
5. to bar from participation **exclude**

■ **Context Clues** Complete each sentence with a list word.

6. Be sure to **include** a title page with your report.
7. The novel is about a British **undercover** agent in World War I.
8. The pond will **overflow** if it rains any more.
9. The Laus' new house will **overlook** the canyon.
10. It is wise to **prearrange** a ride home from the party.
11. To **postdate** the check, Amy wrote tomorrow's date on it.

STRATEGIC SPELLING: Building New Words
Make new words by adding one of the prefixes to each of these base words: *ground, load, crowded, water.*

Add over-	Add under-
12. **overload**	14. **underground**
13. **overcrowded**	15. **underwater**

EXTRA PRACTICE ■ 27

Word List

pretrial	prearrange	postdate	postwar
overcook	overlook	overflow	undercover
include	exclude	premeditated	prehistoric
precaution	postponement	postgraduate	overpopulated
undernourished	underweight	inhale	exhale

■ **Hints** Write the list word that each phrase makes you think of.

1. too many people in a small space
2. wearing a disguise
3. puff out air
4. working together after fighting
5. burn a meal
6. set up a schedule
7. smell a rose
8. going past college graduation
9. lawyers meeting before a hearing
10. too few fruits and vegetables
11. a tool from stone age times

1. **overpopulated**
2. **undercover**
3. **exhale**
4. **postwar**
5. **overcook**
6. **prearrange**
7. **inhale**
8. **postgraduate**
9. **pretrial**
10. **undernourished**
11. **prehistoric**

■ **Puzzle** Write list words in the blanks to match the definitions. The letters in the circle will spell the answer to the question.

12. write a later date **p o s t d a t e**
13. too thin **u n d e r w e i g h t**
14. fail to see **o v e r l o o k**
15. a putting off **p o s t p o n e m e n t**
16. foresight **p r e c a u t i o n**
17. contain **i n c l u d e**
18. flood **o v e r f l o w**
19. planned ahead **p r e m e d i t a t e d**
20. leave out **e x c l u d e**

Which part of an unfamiliar word might help you figure out its meaning?
t h e   p r e f i x

---

27 ■ REVIEW

Word List

pretrial	prearrange	postdate	postwar
overcook	overlook	overflow	undercover
include	exclude	premeditated	prehistoric
precaution	postponement	postgraduate	overpopulated
undernourished	underweight	inhale	exhale

■ **Word Meanings** Write the list word that completes each phrase.

1. ___ the fragrance
2. ___ agent
3. ___ animal
4. ___ studies
5. ___ action

■ **Word Math** Complete each equation to make a list word.

6. over + bake = ___
7. pre + warning = ___
8. over + stream = ___
9. pre + set = ___
10. under + fed = ___
11. post + military conflict = ___
12. over + peopled = ___
13. pre + ordeal = ___
14. under + heaviness = ___
15. post + appointment = ___
16. over + glance = ___

■ **Context Clues** Write the list word that completes each sentence. Say each word carefully to help you spell it.

17. When you want to relax, ___ slowly.
18. Try to ___ a student from each homeroom.
19. The ballgame's ___ means a double-header tomorrow.
20. Budgeting families are trying to ___ as much as possible from shopping lists.

1. **inhale**
2. **undercover**
3. **prehistoric**
4. **postgraduate**
5. **premeditated**
6. **overcook**
7. **precaution**
8. **overflow**
9. **prearrange**
10. **undernourished**
11. **postwar**
12. **overpopulated**
13. **pretrial**
14. **underweight**
15. **postdate**
16. **overlook**
17. **exhale**
18. **include**
19. **postponement**
20. **exclude**

CHALLENGE ■ 28

Challenge Words		
intercept	interception	individual
individuality	cooperate	cooperation

■ Complete the following sentences using the correct forms of the Challenge Words.

1. Each person is an **individual** _____. Our clothes, our faces, and even the way we walk show our **individuality** _____.

2. Since you volunteered to take part in this clean-up, I expect **cooperation** _____. I hope you all intend to **cooperate** _____ fully.

3. Coach, that was an **interception** _____! I saw her **intercept** _____ the ball!

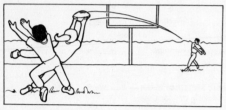

■ In most cases, working together helps to get a project done. Write a paragraph describing the way people work together to accomplish a goal. Use one or more Challenge Words.

_____

_____

_____

_____

_____

_____

107

---

28 ■ THINK AND PRACTICE

direct	direction	history	historical	fact
factual	critic	criticize	produce	production

■ **Word Relationships** Write the list word that matches each clue. Then write the list word that is related to it.

the study of past events

1. **history** _____ 2. **historical** _____

something that can be proven true or false

3. **fact** _____ 4. **factual** _____

one who evaluates a movie, play, or other work of art

5. **critic** _____ 6. **criticize** _____

■ **Related Pairs** To complete each sentence, write two list words that are related.

After going in the wrong (7) **direction** _____, we asked Amy

to (8) **direct** _____ us.

A good art (9) **critic** _____ can (10) **criticize** _____

a work in a constructive way.

It is hard work to (11) **produce** _____ a brand-new musical

(12) **production** _____.

STRATEGIC SPELLING: Seeing Meaning Connections
Complete the paragraph with words from the box.

Words related to *produce*		
product	producer	unproductive

The motion-picture (13) **producer** _____ was upset. He had

watched the movie crew spend an (14) **unproductive** _____ day

trying to shoot an important scene. No one was pleased with the

finished (15) **product** _____. The entire scene would have to

be reshot tomorrow.

108

EXTRA PRACTICE ■ 28

Word List				
direct	direction	history	historical	fact
factual	critic	criticize	produce	production
magic	magician	electric	electrician	distract
distraction	remedy	remedial	origin	original

■ **Making New Words** Write the list word that is formed when you combine the synonym for each word or phrase below with the ending.

1. charged with energy + ian = **electrician** _____

2. guide + ion = **direction** _____

3. source + al = **original** _____

4. disturb + ion = **distraction** _____

5. cure + ial = **remedial** _____

6. make + tion = **production** _____

7. past events + ical = **historical** _____

8. hocus pocus + ian = **magician** _____

9. statistic + ual = **factual** _____

10. reviewer + ize = **criticize** _____

ELECTRICAL WORK

■ **Base Words** Write the list word that is the base word for each word below.

11. origins **origin** _____   16. producing **produce** _____

12. misdirected **direct** _____   17. electrical **electric** _____

13. distracted **distract** _____   18. historian **history** _____

14. magically **magic** _____   19. remedied **remedy** _____

15. factor **fact** _____   20. critical **critic** _____

109

---

28 ■ REVIEW

Word List				
direct	direction	history	historical	fact
factual	critic	criticize	produce	production
magic	magician	electric	electrician	distract
distraction	remedy	remedial	origin	original

■ **Definition Pairs** Write the list words that fit each set of definitions.

1–2. reality/true
3–4. cure/healing
5–6. make/manufacturing
7–8. source/innovative
9–10. divert/interruption
11–12. straight/orientation

1. **fact** _____
2. **factual** _____
3. **remedy** _____
4. **remedial** _____
5. **produce** _____
6. **production** _____
7. **origin** _____
8. **original** _____
9. **distract** _____
10. **distraction** _____
11. **direct** _____
12. **direction** _____

■ **Multiple Meanings** Write the list word that completes each phrase.

13. ancient ___
14. ___ marker
15. my own worst ___
16. ___ era
17. ___ light bulb

13. **history** _____
14. **magic** _____
15. **critic** _____
16. **historical** _____
17. **electric** _____

■ **Drawing Conclusions** Write the list word that answers each question.

18. Who pulls rabbits out of hats?
19. What do reviewers do both positively and negatively?
20. Who keeps currents flowing?

18. **magician** _____
19. **criticize** _____
20. **electrician** _____

110

Everyday Spelling © Scott Foresman • Addison Wesley

Top Left Panel

Name _____

CHALLENGE ■ 29

Challenge Words				
sometimes	some times	backwards	pocketful	underneath

■ Use Challenge Words to complete the puzzle.

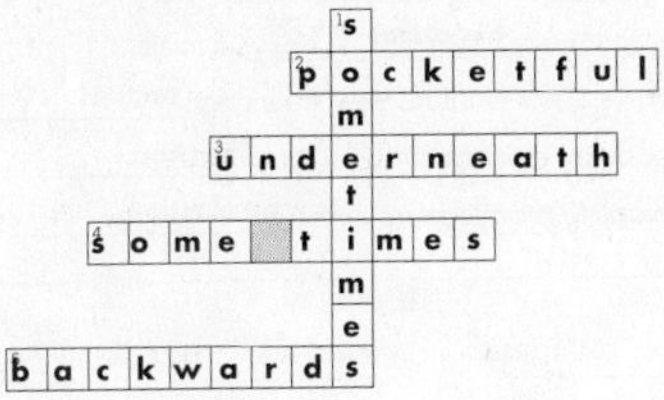

```
            s
  p o c k e t f u l
            m
    u n d e r n e a t h
            t
    s o m e   t i m e s
            m
            e
  b a c k w a r d s
```

Across
2. a filled pouch
3. below
4. certain occasions
5. wrong way around

Down
1. now and then

■ Think about a pocketful of treasures. It could be a collection. It could be a group of lucky charms. Write a description of the treasures using one or more Challenge Words.

_____

_____

_____

_____

_____

_____

_____

111

Top Right Panel

Name _____

29 ■ THINK AND PRACTICE

a lot	want to	all ways	always	away
a way	a little	below	because	together

■ **Antonyms** Write the list word that completes each phrase.

1. not above, but **below** _____
2. not never, but **always** _____
3. not apart, but **together** _____
4. not a little, but **a lot** _____
5. not toward, but **away** _____

■ **Definitions** Write the list word that means the same as the underlined word or words in each sentence.

6. Two violinists performed <u>with one another</u> at the concert. — **together**
7. The gymnasts <u>desire to</u> compete at the Olympics. — **want to**
8. The recipe calls for <u>a tiny bit of</u> hot pepper sauce. — **a little**
9. The club will find <u>a means</u> to raise money for the trip. — **a way**
10. <u>Since</u> she was late, she missed the best part of the play. — **Because**
11. Rosa tried <u>every method</u> of training her dog. — **all ways**
12. Look <u>in another direction</u> when the movie is scary. — **away**

STRATEGIC SPELLING: Seeing Meaning Connections
Write the word that fits each definition.

Words with *way*		
away	always	wayward

13. at all times — **always**
14. resisting authority or control — **wayward**
15. from this or that place — **away**

112

Bottom Left Panel

Name _____

EXTRA PRACTICE ■ 29

Word List				
a lot	want to	all ways	always	away
a way	a little	below	because	together
forget	around	a while	awhile	forever
again	tonight	tomorrow	become	going to

■ **Riddles** Use pairs or groups of confusing words to match the clues below.

1. a teaspoon of sand
2. a beach full of sand
3. the next morning
4. this very evening
5. in cooperation, either time
6. this way, that way, and the other way
7. now, next week, and all the time
8. a circular movement
9. you *gain* when you do something over and over
10. out of sight and at a distance
11. a method
12. a word to tell you about something *lower*
13. a word that means *for this reason*
14. a word that means *come to be,* but turns it around
15. how some people *wish* for action
16. how other people *make a plan* for action
17. the opposite of *remember*
18. a synonym for *always*
19. a time—the object of a preposition
20. also a time—an adverb

1. **a little**
2. **a lot**
3. **tomorrow**
4. **tonight**
5. **together**
6. **all ways**
7. **always**
8. **around**
9. **again**
10. **away**
11. **a way**
12. **below**
13. **because**
14. **become**
15. **want to**
16. **going to**
17. **forget**
18. **forever**
19. **a while**
20. **awhile**

113

Bottom Right Panel

Name _____

29 ■ REVIEW

Word List				
a lot	want to	all ways	always	away
a way	a little	below	because	together
forget	around	a while	awhile	forever
again	tonight	tomorrow	become	going to

■ **Classifying** Write the list word that belongs in each group.

1. yesterday, today, ___
2. desire to, wish to, ___
3. a bit, a smidgen, ___
4. heading for, aiming toward, ___
5. about, approximately, ___
6. a ton, a heap, ___
7. missing, absent, ___
8. develop, evolve, ___
9. over, once more, ___
10. since, whereas, ___
11. every means, total methods, ___
12. a means, a method, ___

■ **Antonyms** Write the list word that means the opposite of each underlined word.

13. The girls decided to go to the dance <u>separately</u>.
14. The recital is taking place <u>today</u>.
15. Sheila did <u>remember</u> to water the lawn.

■ **Multiple Meanings** Write the list word that completes each phrase or sentence.

16. ___ yours
17. Look out ___!
18. Stop in for ___.
19. as ___
20. dream ___ with me

1. **tomorrow**
2. **want to**
3. **a little**
4. **going to**
5. **around**
6. **a lot**
7. **away**
8. **become**
9. **again**
10. **because**
11. **all ways**
12. **a way**
13. **together**
14. **tonight**
15. **forget**
16. **forever**
17. **below**
18. **a while**
19. **always**
20. **awhile**

114

Everyday Spelling © Scott Foresman • Addison Wesley

169

REVIEW ■ 30A

Lesson 25

probably	separate	cabinet	beginning	restaurant

■ **Making Inferences** Write the list word that completes each phrase.

1. not the end or the middle but the **beginning**
2. not a closet or a cupboard but a **cabinet**
3. not definitely or certainly but **probably**
4. not a cafe or a diner but a **restaurant**
5. not joined or together but **separate**

Lesson 26

friendship	championship	attractive	inventive	originate

■ **Word Forms** Write the list word that has each meaning and ending indicated below.

1. winner + ship   **championship**
2. beginning + ate   **originate**
3. draw to + ive   **attractive**
4. someone you like + ship   **friendship**
5. to think up + ive   **inventive**

Lesson 27

overcook	pretrial	postdate	include	exclude

■ **Antonyms** Write the list word that means the opposite of each word.

1. predate   **postdate**
2. exclude   **include**
3. undercook   **overcook**
4. include   **exclude**
5. posttrial   **pretrial**

30B ■ REVIEW

Lesson 28

factual	direction	criticize	historical	production

■ **Context** Write the list word that is related to the underlined word and completes each sentence.

1. It is the job of a <u>critic</u> to **criticize** .
2. I like <u>history</u>, so I read **historical** novels.
3. If you rely on <u>fact</u>, not opinion, you are being **factual** .
4. <u>Direct</u> the hikers by pointing in the right **direction** .
5. Our group plans to <u>produce</u> a musical **production** next fall.

Lesson 29

always	all ways	away	a lot	together

■ **Definitions** Write the list word that fits the definition.

1. at a distance   **away**
2. all directions   **all ways**
3. a great many   **a lot**
4. with each other   **together**
5. at all times   **always**

CHALLENGE ■ 31

Challenge Words
temperamental   parliament   cantaloupe   archaeology   nuisance

■ Write a Challenge Word to match each clue below.

1. a tendency to get angry **temperamental**
2. a kind of melon **cantaloupe**
3. a meeting of lawmakers **parliament**
4. a science about the past **archaeology**
5. a bother **nuisance**

■ Did you ever want to be an archaeologist? Use one or more Challenge Words to write a paragraph comparing and contrasting jobs you might like.

_____
_____
_____
_____
_____
_____
_____
_____
_____

117

---

31 ■ THINK AND PRACTICE

interested	usually	American	toward	business
vegetable	really	opposite	difficult	Christmas

■ **Synonyms** Write the list word that means the same as each word.

1. truly **really**
2. hard **difficult**
3. intrigued **interested**
4. antonym **opposite**
5. trade **business**
6. near **toward**

■ **Analogies** Write the list word that completes each analogy.

7. Peach is to fruit as carrot is to **vegetable**
8. November is to Thanksgiving as December is to **Christmas**
9. Amusement park is to pleasure as office is to **business**
10. Seldom is to infrequently as commonly is to **usually**
11. Italy is to Italian as United States is to **American**
12. Happy is to sad as bored is to **interested**
13. Easy is to simple as troublesome is to **difficult**

STRATEGIC SPELLING: Choosing the Best Strategy
Write two list words that you find hard to spell. Which strategy could help you spell each word? Name the strategy and tell why you chose it. Then compare choices with a partner. For a list of strategies, see page 142.

14. **Answers will vary.** _____

15. **Answers will vary.** _____

118

EXTRA PRACTICE ■ 31

Word List
interested	usually	American	toward	business
vegetable	really	opposite	difficult	Christmas
magazine	apologize	multiply	jealousy	elementary
oxygen	Maryland	sensitive	laughter	disease

■ **Analogies** Write a list word to complete each analogy below.

1. Kiwi is to fruit as eggplant is to ___.
2. Weary is to energetic as bored is to ___.
3. Mexico is to Mexican as America is to ___.
4. *Daily Planet* is to newspaper as *Newsweek* is to ___.
5. Solid is to ice as gas is to ___.
6. Effortless is to simple as laborious is to ___.
7. City is to Baltimore as state is to ___.
8. Add is to subtract as divide is to ___.
9. Jewish is to Hannukah as Christian is to ___.
10. Sadness is to weeping as happiness is to ___.

1. **vegetable**
2. **interested**
3. **American**
4. **magazine**
5. **oxygen**
6. **difficult**
7. **Maryland**
8. **multiply**
9. **Christmas**
10. **laughter**
11. **jealousy**
12. **apologize**
13. **business**
14. **toward**
15. **elementary**
16. **disease**

■ **Hidden Words** Write the list word that matches each description below. Use the underlined word as a clue.

11. You probably feel <u>lousy</u> when you have this emotion.
12. People should not have to do this when they play <u>polo</u>.
13. Do you take a <u>bus</u> to this place?
14. A tugboat has to <u>tow</u> a boat this way to reach shore.
15. Reading is an <u>element</u> of this kind of school.
16. You're not at <u>ease</u> when you have this.

These two words must be friends because they both contain the word <u>ally</u>.

17. **really**   18. **usually**

These two words probably <u>sit</u> around talking about their meanings.

19. **opposite**   20. **sensitive**

119

---

31 ■ REVIEW

Word List
interested	usually	American	toward	business
vegetable	really	opposite	difficult	Christmas
magazine	apologize	multiply	jealousy	elementary
oxygen	Maryland	sensitive	laughter	disease

■ **Definitions** Write the list word that is missing from each person's statement.

1. Scuba diver: "Where are the ___ tanks?"
2. Soldier: "I can fold the ___ flag correctly."
3. Salesperson: "Are you ___ in a wool coat?"
4. Model: "I model in a weekly fashion ___."
5. Doctor: "Finding a cure for that disease is going to be extremely ___."
6. Cadet: "The naval academy is in Annapolis, ___."
7. Teacher: "I've taught all the ___ grades."
8. Mathematician: "Whenever you ___ by zero, you get zero."
9. Poet: "People like my ___ verses about human emotions."
10. Optimist: "I ___, though not always, have high hopes."

1. **oxygen**
2. **American**
3. **interested**
4. **magazine**
5. **difficult**
6. **Maryland**
7. **elementary**
8. **multiply**
9. **sensitive**
10. **usually**
11. **laughter**
12. **disease**
13. **toward**
14. **Christmas**
15. **business**
16. **jealousy**
17. **apologize**
18. **vegetable**
19. **opposite**
20. **really**

■ **Syllables** Each column of letters is one syllable of a two-syllable word. Match the syllables and write the list words.

11. laugh	ness
12. dis	ter
13. to	mas
14. Christ	ease
15. busi	ward

■ **Hidden Words** Each word below is hidden in a list word. Write the list word.

16. lousy   19. site
17. polo   20. real
18. table

120

Page 121

Name _____

CHALLENGE ■ 32

Challenge Words

irrelevant   illiterate   immeasurable   inconsiderate   inequality

■ Write the Challenge Word that goes with each clue below.

1. not able to read   **illiterate**
2. not to the point   **irrelevant**
3. not concerned with fairness   **inequality**
4. not thoughtful   **inconsiderate**
5. not countable   **immeasurable**

■ Imagine that your class has the opportunity to win a trip to the nation's capital. Use Challenge Words to write a paragraph that tells why your class should be chosen for the trip.

_____
_____
_____
_____
_____
_____
_____
_____
_____
_____

121

Page 122

Name _____

32 ■ THINK AND PRACTICE

| illegal | inexpensive | inaccurate | indirect | informal |
| impolite | improper | imperfect | irresponsible | irregular |

■ **Context** Write the list word that is missing from each person's statement.

1. Hostess: "Dress casually for my **informal** party."
2. Salesperson: "This is an **inexpensive** way to update your wardrobe."
3. Parent: "It is **impolite** to forget to write a thank-you note."
4. Police Officer: "It is **illegal** to exceed the speed limit."
5. Mathematician: "The answer to this equation is **inaccurate**."

■ **Synonyms** Write a list word that means about the same as the underlined word or words in each sentence.

6. Drivers will lose their licenses if they are <u>not trustworthy</u>.   **irresponsible**
7. His answer to the teacher's question was <u>not straightforward</u>.   **indirect**
8. The shoes were on sale because they were <u>not made perfectly</u>.   **imperfect**
9. On the map, the coastline looks very <u>uneven</u>.   **irregular**
10. The comedian's joke about his children was <u>in poor taste</u>.   **improper**
11. Amy found a <u>cheap</u> quilt at a garage sale.   **inexpensive**

STRATEGIC SPELLING: Building New Words
Make new words by adding one of the prefixes to each of these words: *active, practical, possible, complete.*
Use your Spelling Dictionary if you need help.

Add in-
12. **inactive**
13. **incomplete**

Add im-
14. **impractical**
15. **impossible**

122

Page 123

Name _____

EXTRA PRACTICE ■ 32

Word List

illegal	inexpensive	inaccurate	indirect	informal
impolite	improper	imperfect	irresponsible	irregular
illogical	illegible	incapable	incredible	impatient
imbalance	immature	irrational	irresistible	irreplaceable

■ **Word Building** All the prefixes in this lesson mean *not*. Write the list word that means the same as each prefix and base word definition below.

1. not + able to do something
2. not + sane
3. not + high-priced
4. not + permitted by law
5. not + suitable
6. not + believable
7. not + grown up
8. not + making sense
9. not + correct
10. not + courteous
11. not + able to be read
12. not + one hundred percent

1. **incapable**
2. **irrational**
3. **inexpensive**
4. **illegal**
5. **improper**
6. **incredible**
7. **immature**
8. **illogical**
9. **inaccurate**
10. **impolite**
11. **illegible**
12. **imperfect**

■ **Making Inferences** Write the list word that each phrase makes you think of.

13. feeling dizzy
14. a lost family heirloom
15. leaving your bike in the way
16. a path that goes a roundabout way
17. pants with different leg lengths
18. wearing casual clothing
19. a cool lake on a hot day
20. wanting to get started immediately

13. **imbalance**
14. **irreplaceable**
15. **irresponsible**
16. **indirect**
17. **irregular**
18. **informal**
19. **irresistible**
20. **impatient**

123

Page 124

Name _____

32 ■ REVIEW

Word List

illegal	inexpensive	inaccurate	indirect	informal
impolite	improper	imperfect	irresponsible	irregular
illogical	illegible	incapable	incredible	impatient
imbalance	immature	irrational	irresistible	irreplaceable

■ **Analogies** Write the list words to complete the analogies.

1. Correct is to right as wrong is to ___.
2. Rich is to costly as cheap is to ___.
3. Sun is to credible as flying saucer is to ___.
4. Law is to legal as speeding is to ___.
5. Quiet is to patient as fidget is to ___
6. Tree is to mature as seed is to ___.
7. Reasonable is to logical as unreasonable is to ___.
8. Same is to rational as crazy is to ___.
9. Top hat is to formal as jeans are to ___.
10. Can is to cannot as capable is to ___.
11. Mannerly is to proper as vulgar is to ___.

1. **inaccurate**
2. **inexpensive**
3. **incredible**
4. **illegal**
5. **impatient**
6. **immature**
7. **illogical**
8. **irrational**
9. **informal**
10. **incapable**
11. **improper**

■ **Building New Words** Make new words by adding the prefix **ir-** to these base words. Use your Spelling Dictionary if you need help.

12. responsible
13. replaceable
14. resistible

12. **irresponsible**
13. **irreplaceable**
14. **irresistible**

■ **Puzzle** Use the clues to help you fill in the puzzle with list words.

Across
2. inequality
4. random
5. rude

Down
1. unreadable
2. defective
3. roundabout

```
          ²i        ³i
²i m b a l a n c e    n
  m       l          d
  p       e          i
  e       g          r
  r      ⁴i r r e g u l a r
  f       b          e
  e       l
  c      ⁵i m p o l i t e
  t       e
```

124

172

Everyday Spelling © Scott Foresman • Addison Wesley

CHALLENGE ■ 33

Challenge Words

significance   incompetence   disinfectant   disobedient   concurrent

■ Use Challenge Words to complete the relationships described below.

1. **Concurrent** _____ is to consecutive as rich is to poor.
2. **Disobedient** _____ is to law-abiding as hungry is to well-fed.
3. **Incompetence** _____ is to excellence as bumbling is to grace.
4. **Disinfectant** _____ is to germs as medicine is to bacteria.
5. **Significance** _____ is to importance as sadness is to gloom.

■ Sometimes, taking responsibility brings more than you bargained for. Use one or more Challenge Words to write a paragraph about a baby-sitting, dog-sitting, or house-sitting job that wasn't as easy as it seemed.

_____
_____
_____
_____
_____
_____
_____
_____
_____
_____
_____
_____

---

33 ■ THINK AND PRACTICE

| entrance | performance | appearance | clearance | independence |
| difference | excellence | brilliant | important | intelligent |

■ **Word Forms** Write the list words that contain these base words.

1. excel — **excellence**
2. depend — **independence**
3. differ — **difference**
4. enter — **entrance**
5. import — **importance**

■ **Definitions** Write the list word that fits each definition.

6. a public presentation — **performance**
7. outward look — **appearance**
8. shining very brightly — **brilliant**
9. a sale to get rid of stock — **clearance**
10. having mental capacity — **intelligent**
11. the act of coming in — **entrance**

STRATEGIC SPELLING: Building New Words
Add the suffix -**ence** or -**ance** to each base word to make a new word. Check the Spelling Dictionary if you need help.

Base word	New word
12. exist	**existence**
13. inherit	**inheritance**
14. refer	**reference**
15. attend	**attendance**

EXTRA PRACTICE ■ 33

Word List

entrance	performance	appearance	clearance
independence	difference	excellence	brilliant
important	intelligent	insurance	confidence
coincidence	pollutant	ignorant	hesitant
apparent	persistent	convenient	consistent

■ **Pronunciations** Write a list word for each pronunciation.

1. (kən vē′nyənt)
2. (im pôrt′nt)
3. (kon′fə dəns)
4. (bril′yənt)
5. (ə par′ənt)
6. (in tel′ə jənt)
7. (kən sis′tənt)
8. (ig′nər ənt)
9. (kō in′sə dəns)
10. (in′di pen′dəns)

1. **convenient**
2. **important**
3. **confidence**
4. **brilliant**
5. **apparent**
6. **intelligent**
7. **consistent**
8. **ignorant**
9. **coincidence**
10. **independence**

■ **Word Forms** Write the list word that belongs in each group.

11. hesitate, hesitated, ___
12. appear, disappear, ___
13. clearly, unclear, ___
14. persisted, persistence, ___
15. differ, different, ___
16. insured, uninsured, ___
17. entry, entering, ___
18. excelling, excellent, ___
19. unpolluted, polluting, ___
20. perform, performing, ___

11. **hesitant**
12. **appearance**
13. **clearance**
14. **persistent**
15. **difference**
16. **insurance**
17. **entrance**
18. **excellence**
19. **pollutant**
20. **performance**

---

33 ■ REVIEW

Word List

entrance	performance	appearance	clearance
independence	difference	excellence	brilliant
important	intelligent	insurance	confidence
coincidence	pollutant	ignorant	hesitant
apparent	persistent	convenient	consistent

■ **Word Forms** Combine each base word below with either a suffix or a suffix and prefix to write a list word.

1. clear
2. import
3. persist
4. appear
5. depend
6. excel
7. consist
8. perform
9. confide
10. coincide
11. differ

1. **clearance**
2. **important**
3. **persistent**
4. **appearance**
5. **independence**
6. **excellence**
7. **consistent**
8. **performance**
9. **confidence**
10. **coincidence**
11. **difference**

■ **Antonyms** Write the list word that completes each phrase.

12. not *knowing*, but ___
13. not *camouflaged*, but ___
14. not *exit*, but ___
15. not *certain*, but ___
16. not *out-of-the-way*, but ___
17. not *purifier*, but ___
18. not *dark*, but ___
19. not *stupid*, but ___
20. not *risk*, but ___

12. **ignorant**
13. **apparent**
14. **entrance**
15. **hesitant**
16. **convenient**
17. **pollutant**
18. **brilliant**
19. **intelligent**
20. **insurance**

CHALLENGE ■ 34

Challenge Words		
vice-president	great-grandfather	warm-blooded
bookkeeper	headstrong	

■ Write the Challenge Words for each clue listed.

1. This one can help you count your money. **bookkeeper**
2. This one can help your country. **vice-president**
3. This one can help you learn about your family. **great-grandfather**
4. All mammals are like this. **warm-blooded**
5. All stubborn people are like this. **headstrong**

■ America is full of exciting success stories. Use one or more Challenge Words to write a paragraph about an inventor, explorer, artist, or business person you admire. Tell why you think that person is inspiring.

_____
_____
_____
_____
_____
_____
_____
_____
_____
_____
_____

34 ■ THINK AND PRACTICE

basketball	everywhere	outside	summertime	something
baby-sit	roller-skating	drive-in	self-control	part-time

■ **Associations** Write the list word that is associated with each item.

1. self-discipline **self-control**
2. nature **outside**
3. gymnasium **basketball**
4. August **summertime**
5. rink **roller-skating**

■ **Drawing Conclusions** Write the list word that answers each question.

6. What is your work schedule if it is not full-time? **part-time**
7. How might you earn money from a family with small children? **baby-sit**
8. Where could you eat a hamburger in your car? **drive-in**
9. Where would you travel if you went all over the world? **everywhere**
10. When does the sun shine the longest? **summertime**
11. What would you have if you didn't have nothing? **something**
12. What's one way to get around on wheels? **roller-skating**

STRATEGIC SPELLING: Seeing Meaning Connections
Complete the passage with words from the box.

Words with *drive*		
driver	driveway	drive-in

My older brother is a new (13) **driver**. On Saturday, he offered to take me to the (14) **drive-in** burger place for lunch. I didn't breathe easily until we were back safely in our own (15) **driveway**!

EXTRA PRACTICE ■ 34

Word List			
basketball	everywhere	outside	summertime
something	baby-sit	roller-skating	drive-in
self-control	part-time	afterthought	cheerleader
quarterback	bookstore	courthouse	ice-skated
ninety-five	brother-in-law	water-skied	old-fashioned

■ **Word Math** Write a list word to match each equation.

1. huddle + signals + football =
2. hoop + dribble + court =
3. ninety + three + two =
4. sister + husband + relative =
5. yells + jumping + uniform =
6. food + window + car =
7. business + reading + buy =
8. infant + care + job =
9. sport + water + towing =
10. lawyers + judge + place =
11. firmness + will power + determination =
12. sport + sidewalk + fast-moving =

1. **quarterback**
2. **basketball**
3. **ninety-five**
4. **brother-in-law**
5. **cheerleader**
6. **drive-in**
7. **bookstore**
8. **baby-sit**
9. **water-skied**
10. **courthouse**
11. **self-control**
12. **roller-skating**

■ **Find the Compound** Find two words in each sentence that make up a compound word from the list and write the word.

13. Put these boxes out on the porch on the side away from the weather.
14. She fell on the ice, but then got up and skated away.
15. Every time you lose your hat you ask me where it is!
16. This old rocker was fashioned in 1912.
17. After they went, I thought of something I should have told them.
18. Each summer we make time to visit Grandpa.
19. We'll spend part of Saturday doing chores and the rest of the time hiking.
20. Some days I can't get a thing done.

13. **outside**
14. **ice-skated**
15. **everywhere**
16. **old-fashioned**
17. **afterthought**
18. **summertime**
19. **part-time**
20. **something**

34 ■ REVIEW

Word List			
basketball	everywhere	outside	summertime
something	baby-sit	roller-skating	drive-in
self-control	part-time	afterthought	cheerleader
quarterback	bookstore	courthouse	ice-skated
ninety-five	brother-in-law	water-skied	old-fashioned

■ **Hidden Words** Each word below is hidden in a list word. Write the list word.

1. though
2. our
3. ask
4. elf
5. lead
6. thin
7. here
8. net

1. **afterthought**
2. **courthouse**
3. **basketball**
4. **self-control**
5. **cheerleader**
6. **something**
7. **everywhere**
8. **ninety-five**
9. **summertime**
10. **roller-skating**
11. **baby-sit**
12. **old-fashioned**
13. **bookstore**
14. **part-time**
15. **quarterback**
16. **ice-skated**
17. **outside**
18. **drive-in**
19. **water-skied**
20. **brother-in-law**

■ **Riddles** Write the list word that answers each riddle.

9. When is all the time a hot time?
10. What's an eight-wheeling sport?
11. What do you do when you sit for, not on?
12. Which fashion is never trendy?
13. Where can you buy shelved ideas?
14. What kind of time is never whole?
15. What's one-fourth of a fullback?

■ **Analogies** Write the list word that completes each phrase.

16. Arena is to wrestled as rink is to ___.
17. Inner is to inside as outer is to ___.
18. Movie is to theater as fast-food is to ___.
19. Helmet is to bicycled as life jacket is to ___.
20. Aunt is to uncle as sister-in-law is to ___.

CHALLENGE ■ 35

Challenge Words
telecommunication xylophone autonomy cacophony deportation

■ Answer the following questions using Challenge Words.

1. Which word "plugs you in"? __telecommunication__

2. Which sound is always overwhelming? __cacophony__

3. Which word sends you away? __deportation__

4. Which word shows independence? __autonomy__

5. Which sound vibrates clearly? __xylophone__

■ Almost everyone has heard a sound that is loud and awful. Use one or more Challenge Words to write a description of your "terrible sound."

_____
_____
_____
_____
_____
_____
_____
_____

133

35 ■ THINK AND PRACTICE

automobile	autograph	telescope	telecast	telephone
microphone	headphones	portable	import	export

■ **Analogies** Write the list word that completes each analogy.

1. Germs are to microscope as stars are to __telescope__

2. Fly is to airplane as drive is to __automobile__

3. Radio is to broadcast as television is to __telecast__

4. Picture is to photograph as signature is to __autograph__

5. Write is to typewriter as call is to __telephone__.

■ **Context** Write the list word that completes each sentence.

6. Ryan listened to music on his __headphones__ while he mowed the lawn.

7. Albert bought a small, __portable__ television set for his room.

8. Many South American countries __export__ coffee beans to other nations.

9. Talk directly into the __microphone__ when you give your speech.

10. The United States must __import__ much fuel oil from other countries.

STRATEGIC SPELLING: Seeing Meaning Connections

headlight	headstrong	headline	headband

11. Write a list word that is related to the words in the box.   __headphones__

Write the words from the box that fit the definitions.

12. hard to control or manage   __headstrong__

13. cloth or ribbon worn around the head   __headband__

14. a bright light at the front of a vehicle   __headlight__

15. words in heavy type at the top of an article   __headline__

134

EXTRA PRACTICE ■ 35

Word List			
automobile	autograph	telescope	telecast
telephone	microphone	headphones	portable
import	export	automatic	autobiography
autopilot	telegram	telegraph	symphony
saxophone	megaphone	transport	passport

■ **Analogies** Write a list word to complete each analogy below.

1. Taxi is to taxicab as auto is to ___.
2. Car is to license as travel is to ___.
3. Celebrity is to hero as signature is to ___.
4. Other is to biography as self is to ___.
5. String is to violin as reed is to ___.
6. Bugs are to microscope as stars are to ___.
7. Heavy is to stationary as light is to ___.
8. Coach is to team as conductor is to ___.
9. Hotel is to motel as broadcast is to ___.
10. Fridge is to refrigerator as phone is to ___.

■ **Definitions** Use list words to complete each paragraph.

These devices all have to do with sound. An engineer wears an _(11)_ during a recording session. A plugged-in _(12)_ allows the human voice to reach a crowd. A _(13)_ can do the same thing but without electricity.

These words all have to do with carrying. An _(14)_ is something carried or sent out of a country. An _(15)_ is brought into a country. The _(16)_ is the method by which the item is carried. This may be a train, a boat, or a plane.

These words have to do with distance. A _(17)_ is a message that comes over a long distance. The _(18)_ is the technological device that carries the message.

These words have to do with things that can move by themselves. A device allows a plane to be guided by itself, without needing a human pilot. It is called an _(19)_. The word is a combination of the words _(20)_ and *pilot*.

1. __automobile__
2. __passport__
3. __autograph__
4. __autobiography__
5. __saxophone__
6. __telescope__
7. __portable__
8. __symphony__
9. __telecast__
10. __telephone__
11. __headphones__
12. __microphone__
13. __megaphone__
14. __export__
15. __import__
16. __transport__
17. __telegram__
18. __telegraph__
19. __autopilot__
20. __automatic__

135

35 ■ REVIEW

Word List			
automobile	autograph	telescope	telecast
telephone	microphone	headphones	portable
import	export	automatic	autobiography
autopilot	telegram	telegraph	symphony
saxophone	megaphone	transport	passport

■ **Associations** Write the list word that is associated with each item below.

1. movie star
2. tires
3. voyage to other countries
4. pep rally
5. ear receivers
6. planet
7. music conductor
8. Morse code machine
9. own story
10. truck fleet
11. TV show
12. electronic bank teller
13. ringing device

■ **Definitions** Write the list word that matches each clue.

14. What is a product we buy from another nation?
15. What instrument is named after Adolphe Sax?
16. What's a battery-run TV?
17. What is a wired message?
18. What is a product we sell to another nation?
19. What does an emcee speak into?
20. What helps a jet fly on its own?

1. __autograph__
2. __automobile__
3. __passport__
4. __megaphone__
5. __headphones__
6. __telescope__
7. __symphony__
8. __telegraph__
9. __autobiography__
10. __transport__
11. __telecast__
12. __automatic__
13. __telephone__
14. __import__
15. __saxophone__
16. __portable__
17. __telegram__
18. __export__
19. __microphone__
20. __autopilot__

136

175

Lesson 31

interested	toward	usually	difficult	business

■ **Antonyms** Write the list word that means the opposite of each word or phrase.

1. easy **difficult**
2. away from **toward**
3. bored **interested**
4. pleasure **business**
5. rarely **usually**

Lesson 32

illegal	inexpensive	impolite	imperfect	irregular

■ **Definitions** Write the list word that means the same as the underlined words.

1. A shirt that is not costly is **inexpensive** .
2. An action not within the law is **illegal** .
3. When something is not exactly right, it is said to be **imperfect** .
4. If someone is not mannerly, that person may be **impolite** .
5. A heart with a beat that is not steady has an **irregular** beat.

Lesson 33

entrance	appearance	independence	brilliant	intelligent

■ **Word Forms** Write the list word that has each meaning and suffix indicated below.

Meaning	Suffix	List word
1. freedom from	-ence	**independence**
2. a place to go in	-ance	**entrance**
3. brightly shining	-ant	**brilliant**
4. how one looks	-ance	**appearance**
5. very smart	-ent	**intelligent**

Lesson 34

outside	everywhere	summertime	drive-in	part-time

■ **Compounds** Find the two words in each sentence that make up a compound word from the list and write the word.

1. I part my hair in the middle some of the time. **part-time**
2. Every pupil wondered where the teacher was. **everywhere**
3. Summer is a wonderful time to read. **summertime**
4. We will take a drive in the country. **drive-in**
5. Put the dog out in the side yard. **outside**

Lesson 35

autograph	telescope	export	portable	headphones

■ **Seeing Relationships** Write the list word or words that match each clue.

1. Has the Greek word part *auto* meaning "self"

2. Has the Latin root *phon* meaning "voice" or "sound"

3. Has the Greek word part *tele* meaning "far off"

4.–5. Have the Latin root *port* meaning "to carry"

1. **autograph**
2. **headphones**
3. **telescope**
4. **export**
5. **portable**